KE...

THE UNOFFICIAL GUIDE TO

BASKETBALL'S

NASTIEST AND

MOST UNUSUAL RECORDS

GREY*STONE* BOOKS

Douglas & McIntyre Publishing Group

Vancouver/Toronto/Berkeley

For Boomer, who was there for every word.

Copyright © 2005 by Kerry Banks

05 06 07 08 09 5 4 3 2 1

Greystone Books
A division of Douglas & McIntyre Ltd.
2323 Quebec Street, Suite 201
Vancouver, British Columbia V5T 4S7
www.greystonebooks.com

Library and Archives Canada Cataloguing in Publication
Banks, Kerry, 1952–
The unofficial guide to basketball's nastiest and
most unusual records / Kerry Banks.
Includes index.

ISBN-13: 978-1-55365-122-2   ISBN-10: 1-55365-122-7

1. Basketball—Miscellanea. I. Title.
GV885.B36 2005   796.323   C2005-903639-7

Library of Congress Information is available upon request.

Editing by Ruth Wilson
Cover and interior design by Jessica Sullivan
Cover photograph by Walter Smith/CORBIS
Printed and bound in Canada by Friesens
Distributed in the U.S. by Publishers Group West

We gratefully acknowledge the financial support of the Canada Council for the Arts, the British Columbia Arts Council, and the Government of Canada through the Book Publishing Industry Development Program (BPIDP) for our publishing activities.

KERRY BANKS *is an award-winning magazine journalist and the author of 14 other sports books, including* Pavel Bure: The Riddle of the Russian Rocket.

CONTENTS

INTRODUCTION

There is nasty and then there is nasty. The word can certainly be used to describe the brawl at Detroit's Palace of the Auburn Hills that erupted November 19, 2004, when Indiana's Ron Artest waded into the seats to slug it out with drunken fans. Artest received a 72-game suspension for his vicious outburst, an NBA record for an on-court incident. Then, too, there is the sort of nastiness that results in an in-court appearance, such as the October 2004 arrest of Portland Trial Blazers forward Qyntel Woods for staging dogfights at his home, an unwanted first for an NBA player.

Nasty can also apply to an imposing athletic feat, such as Kobe Bryant nailing a record 12 shots from beyond the arc against Seattle in January 2003, or Wilt Chamberlain hauling down a record 55 rebounds in a game against Boston in November 1960. Both accomplishments are amazing on their own, but when you consider the circumstances in which they were achieved, they slip into the realm of supernatural. When Bryant set his record, he was under indictment for rape and was facing a possible 20 years behind bars. Chamberlain set his glass-cleaning mark playing heads-up against Bill

Russell, the Celtics rebounding wizard who held the record of 51 boards that Chamberlain broke that night.

You will find large doses of both types of nastiness in the following pages, as well as a lot of simply strange stuff, such as the records for the most games played by a virgin, the largest fine for kicking a photographer in the testicles, the longest piece of biblical scripture tattooed on a player's body, and the longest game delay caused by a bat.

Most of these records have been culled from the NBA, in part because of its rich and dramatic history, but also because the league is such fertile ground for outrageous and extreme behavior. The road to the finals is paved with weirdness. I hope you enjoy the trip.

KERRY BANKS
May 2005

[1]

RIM
ROCKERS

Darryl Dawkins, a six-foot-eleven, 260-pound wrecking ball known as "Chocolate Thunder," loved the power dunk. "When I dunk, I put something on it. I want the ball to hit the floor before I do," said Dawkins. So that's where we begin, going to the hoop hard with glass-rattling records.

Most stupendous dunk in a game

Vince Carter, Team USA, September 25, 2000

Stephon Marbury once said about Vince Carter: "You can write anything you want to write about him. Anything you got in your mind as far as what you can imagine, you can write. In a game, in a competition—he's the greatest dunker I've ever seen." The Carter legend grew with one giant leap at the 2000 Sydney Olympics. In a game against France he stole a pass, then dribbled toward the basket where seven-foot-two Frederic Weis stood in his path. Vinsanity didn't try to dribble around Weis. Instead he took off from a step or two inside the foul line, spread his legs in midair and went right over Weis, barely scraping the top of the Frenchman's buzz cut, before powering the ball home. The death dunk, they called it.

Most dramatic slam dunk contest

Michael Jordan vs. Dominique Wilkins, February 6, 1988

The game's two greatest skywalkers faced off in the 1988 NBA slam dunk finals in front of a packed Chicago Stadium crowd. With a dazzling blend of power and finesse, Wilkins, the man they dubbed the "Human Highlight Film," took a comfortable lead heading into the fourth and final dunk after earning two straight perfect scores of 50 points. But Wilkins's two-handed windmill jam scored a modest 45, leaving the door open to Jordan, who needed a 49 to win. MJ decided to attempt to dunk from the foul line, a feat that had only been accomplished once before—by Julius Erving at the very first dunk competition at the 1976 ABA All-Star game. By coincidence, Erving happened to be in attendance in Chicago. "I looked up into the box seats and came across the guy who started it all, Dr. J," Jordan said afterward. "He told me to go back all the way, go the length of the floor, then take off from the free-throw line. It was the best advice I got all night." With the cheering crowd on its feet, Jordan started off running, dribbled four times, then elevated from the free-throw line, hanging in the air for what seemed like an eternity, before ramming the ball through the hoop. The judges awarded him a perfect 50 and the title.

Shortest player to win a slam dunk contest

Spud Webb, Atlanta, February 3, 1986

At five-foot-seven and 135 pounds, Webb was one of the smallest men to play in the NBA. Lightning fast and a slick shooter and passer, he defied the odds by playing 12 years in a world of giants. But Webb's most lasting legacy was his improbable victory in the 1986 NBA dunk contest in Dallas. The pint-sized Texan stunned the crowd at Reunion Arena, defeating defending champion and Atlanta Hawks teammate Dominique Wilkins by scoring two perfect 50s in the final round.

First NBA player to break a backboard

Chuck Connors, Boston, November 5, 1946

Connors, who would later go on to much greater fame as the star of TV's *The Rifleman,* broke the backboard at Boston Arena before the Celtics' maiden home opener against the Chicago Stags. Contrary to popular belief he did not do it with a dunk. "During the warm-ups, I took a harmless 15- to 20-foot set shot, and, crash, the glass backboard shattered," Connors recalled in a 1986 interview. The backboard crumbled because a worker had not installed a piece of protective rubber between it and the rim. The game was delayed an hour while a truck picked up a spare backboard from Boston Garden, where a rodeo was playing to a packed house. In 53 career games with the Celtics, Connors averaged 4.5 points per game. After leaving basketball he tried his hand at baseball, playing briefly for the Brooklyn Dodgers and Chicago Cubs, before finding his niche in Hollywood.

Most backboards broken, one game

2: Charlie "Helicopter" Hentz, Pittsburgh Condors (ABA), November 6, 1970

Hentz played only one ABA season with the Pittsburgh Condors, but that was enough for him to set this record. In a 1970 game against the Carolina Cougars, the monster leaper shattered the backboard on a dunk at Dorton Arena in Raleigh. The game was delayed while a wooden one was located in storage. With 67 seconds left, Hentz imploded the other backboard. The game was halted and Carolina was declared a 122–107 victor.

Most stab wounds suffered by a player

11: Paul Pierce, Boston, September 25, 2000

Pierce was definitely in the wrong place at the wrong time. He was also more than a little lucky. Minutes after entering a Boston dance club in the early morning hours of September 25, 2000, the 22-year-old Celtics player was ambushed after he stopped to chat with a gang member's sister. Jumped from behind by three men, he was sucker punched, had a bottle broken over his right eye, and had a knife plunged through the back of his leather jacket six inches into his body. Pierce also received 10 other stab wounds in the neck and chest, the worst of which penetrated his abdomen and diaphragm

and punctured his lung, coming within an inch of his heart.
His friends rushed him to hospital where he underwent
emergency surgery to repair the damage. Amazingly, Pierce
was back on the court in less than a month and went on to
have a stellar season, leading the Celtics in scoring.

Highest draft pick to die of a drug overdose
Len Bias, No. 2 overall, June 19, 1986
Bias was considered a can't-miss star. Not only was the
22-year-old a terrific talent, he also had a sterling reputation.
As his college coach Lefty Driesell stated, "Leonard's only
vice is ice cream." Unfortunately, the Maryland Terrapins
forward never got a chance to strut his stuff in the pros. Less
than 48 hours after being selected second overall by the
Boston Celtics, Bias collapsed in his dorm and died of a
cardiac arrest. Doctors found cocaine in Bias's system and
concluded that he died of a cocaine-induced seizure. A subsequent investigation into his death led to charges being laid
against three other people who admitted using the drug with
Bias on the day of his death. The fallout eventually resulted
in Driesell's resignation.

Most serious injury suffered in a game
Brain damage: Maurice Stokes, Cincinnati, March 12, 1958
Stokes's life took a tragic turn in Minneapolis on March 12,
1958, when he drove to the basket, drew contact, and fell
awkwardly to the floor, hitting his head. Knocked out for
several minutes, he was revived with smelling salts and returned to the game. Three days later, the Royals lost their
playoff opener at Detroit, and after a 12-point, 15-rebound
performance, Stokes became ill on the flight back to Cincinnati. "I feel like I'm going to die," he told a teammate. When

the plane landed, he was taken to a hospital in Covington, Kentucky, where it was determined that the 24-year-old had suffered a brain injury that had damaged his motor control. His life, however, wasn't over, thanks to teammate Jack Twyman who helped to raise money for his medical expenses and became his legal guardian. Though his body suffered spasms and his fingers didn't always function, Stokes learned how to type again and how to paint. He died at age 36 in 1970.

First player to sue a rival team for inflicting an injury

Rudy Tomjanovich, Houston, 1977

During a game on December 9, 1977, Kermit Washington of the Lakers and Kevin Kunnert of the Rockets got into a fight. Rudy Tomjanovich left the Houston bench and rushed to help his teammate, but as he arrived on the scene, Washington wheeled and delivered a crushing blow. The punch shattered most of the bones in Tomjanovich's face and actually knocked the top half of his skull out of alignment with the bottom half. He suffered a concussion and lacerations and was leaking spinal fluid into his nose. Tomjanovich was hospitalized for weeks and missed the rest of the season. He returned the next year after five facial surgeries, but was never the same player. Tomjanovich sued the Lakers and won a $3.2-million award. Washington, who was fined $10,000 and suspended for 60 days, was never the same player after the incident either.

First player sued because of a dog bite

Tracy McGrady, Houston, January 2005

When McGrady returned to play in Orlando for the first time since an off-season trade to Houston, reporters wanted to ask him about his dog, Max. The Rockets guard had just been sued by a man who claimed that he lost the tip of his nose when McGrady's Rottweiler attacked him on August 25, 2004, at the player's Florida mansion. Fred Chamberlin, who was employed by McGrady at the time as a home maintenance engineer, said he was attacked on the second floor of the house after climbing a flight of stairs. When Max jumped him, the 57-year-old Chamberlin fell backward down the stairs, leaving him with a ringing in his ears. McGrady admitted that Max is a "very vicious dog," but said that he is usually nice. "I feel terrible," McGrady said. "I didn't think he had it in him."

First player suspended for biting another player
Wayne "Tree" Rollins, Atlanta, April 24, 1983
Boston was leading the deciding game of its 1983 playoff series with Atlanta when Tree Rollins elbowed Danny Ainge. The feisty Celtics guard responded by tackling the seven-foot-one Hawks center. As the two struggled on the floor, Rollins sank his teeth into one of Ainge's fingers, opening a gash that required five stitches. The NBA handed Rollins a five-game suspension, one game for each stitch. The next day's headline in Boston read: "Tree Bites Man."

First player to return to action after undergoing a kidney transplant
Sean Elliott, San Antonio, March 2000
Elliott was diagnosed in 1993 with a progressive kidney disorder. He began treatment with medication, but his condition gradually deteriorated. By March 1999 doctors told him to prepare for the inevitable—transplant or dialysis. Then in August, Elliott's brother Noel came up with a critical assist, donating one of his kidneys to the star forward. Miraculously,

Elliott returned to action on March 14, 2000, and went on to play 71 games over two seasons after his transplant.

First player sidelined by playing too many video games
Lionel Simmons, Sacramento, 1990–91

Shortly after being named Player of the Week in 1990–91, "L-Train" missed two games due to tendonitis in his wrists from overexposure to his Game Boy. Simmons may have been the first Nintendo casualty, but he wasn't the last. The next season Seattle's Derrick McKey went down for seven games with the same affliction.

Most bizarre excuse for missing a season opener
Burned corneas: Charles Barkley, Phoenix, November 1994

Barkley missed the opening game of the 1994–95 season with one of the most unbelievable ailments of all time. Apparently the stage lights at an Eric Clapton concert he attended were too bright, causing him to rub his eyes. A nasty chemical reaction occurred due to the hand lotion Barkley had been using, and he burned the first layer of his corneas.

Most unusual reason for being placed on the injured list
Insomnia: Moochie Norris, Seattle, March 4, 1999

This was the real Sleepless in Seattle. Many people laughed when Norris was placed on the injured list because of insomnia by the Sonics in 1999, but it wasn't funny to Norris. The NBA guard, who got the nickname "Moochie" from his grandfather, a fan of the Cab Calloway classic "Minnie the Moocher," had suffered from insomnia since his mother died of cancer in 1989. Unable to get more than two hours of shut-eye a night, Norris had tried various cures. In 1998 while toiling for the Fort Wayne Fury in the CBA, he went to bed wearing glasses that flashed lights and emitted a thumping sound when he closed his eyes. (The thinking was that he'd focus on the noise and lights and clear his mind.) Seattle decided that Norris was a head case. The team waived him a couple of days after he went on the injured list.

First player sidelined by a luggage cart

Jeff Ruland, Philadelphia, 1991–92

Ruland had been retired for four seasons with nagging knee injuries when he tried to make a comeback with Philadelphia in 1991–92. His comeback ended after 13 games when a luggage cart rammed into him as he waited for a team bus outside Boston Garden. The collision left him with a partially torn Achilles tendon. An exasperated Ruland exclaimed, "It can't be accidental, they were moving too fast. Whoever could foresee anything like this happening?"

Most preposterous use of a basketball card

For personal identification: Qyntel Woods, Portland, 2002

In March 2002 Woods was stopped by police for speeding. As he rolled down the window of his Cadillac Escalade, marijuana fumes poured out. The police searched the vehicle and found a small amount of grass. When the Trail Blazers rookie was asked for his driver's license and proof of insurance, he had neither. Instead, he handed the officers his basketball card as identification. He was charged with marijuana possession and driving without a license and no proof of insurance. Woods provided proof of insurance in July to lift the suspension, but his license was suspended again on July 28 when he failed to appear at his court hearing. Seven months later, Woods was stopped again by the same police officer for failing to use his turn signals. In a bad case of déjà vu, he was booked for driving with a suspended license and no proof of insurance. Fortunately, this time Woods wasn't enveloped in a cloud of ganja.

Most exaggerated example of personal hardship

Buying a house: Kevin Garnett, Minnesota, October 2002
Are NBA stars out of touch with reality? Garnett, for one, would appear to be. In an 2002 *GQ* interview, the Timberwolves forward, who signed a six-year, $126-million contract in 1997, remarked: "The things I have been through since I came into the NBA, you would not believe how hard it has been." Asked to cite an example, Garnett replied, "Buying my first house. That was a hardship."

Most pre-game vomiting episodes, career

1,128: Bill Russell, 1956–57 to 1968–69
The Boston Celtics great would get so psyched—and nauseated—before virtually every game that he would have to puke. It didn't hurt his play though. In fact, if Russell didn't vomit before a game, his teammates knew they were in for a long night. Once, before a Game 7 playoff clash against Philadelphia in the 1960s, Celtics coach Red Auerbach actually pulled his team off the court during warm-ups because Russell hadn't performed his usual pre-game ritual. Auerbach told the players they weren't going back out until Russell tossed his cookies. Russell came through and Boston went on to victory.

Only player to credit LSD with improving his play

Phil Jackson, New York, 1973–74

Jackson was an unconventional dude long before he became one of the NBA's most celebrated coaches. In his 1975 book *Maverick: More Than a Game,* Jackson claimed that some LSD he gobbled for breakfast in Malibu in May 1973 lent his game a boost. The shaggy-haired Knicks forward said the "spiritual flash" he experienced that day on the beach gave him a new love for the sport and a deeper appreciation of team play. He credited it with making 1973–74 the most productive season of his career, as he averaged 11.1 points and 5.8 rebounds per game.

First player to order takeout during a game

Quintin Dailey, Chicago, March 20, 1985

During the second half of a game against the Spurs in San Antonio, Dailey instructed the ball boy to borrow five dollars from a reporter and run to the concession stand for a slice of pizza. When the ball boy returned, Dailey took the pizza and ate it at the end of the bench, much to the amusement of his teammates and the astonishment of coach Kevin Loughery.

Only NBA player to kill a lion with a spear

Manute Bol, 1985–86 to 1994–95

One thing is beyond dispute: Manute Bol is the greatest seven-foot-seven center from Sudan to play in the NBA. At 15, the Dinka herdsman killed a marauding lion with his spear while it lay sleeping—a feat his agent noted during his contract negotiations. Bol was first handed a basketball at age 19 and told to try to dunk it. On his initial attempt he smashed several of his teeth on the rim. But he persevered and soon became much sought after by American colleges despite being, like everyone in his tribe, illiterate. In his first NBA season, Bol blocked 397 shots, the second-highest total of all time.

Only NBA player raised in a Japanese concentration camp
Tom Meschery, 1961–62 to 1970–71
A fierce competitor who earned the nickname "the Mad Russian" during a 10-year NBA career, Meschery was the first Golden State Warrior to have his number retired. No other player had such an unusual childhood. His Russian parents fled the aftermath of the Bolshevik Revolution, eventually settling in Harbin, China, where Tom was born in 1938. Meschery's father later immigrated to the U.S., where he found work in a San Francisco shipyard. The family planned to join him there, but before they could depart the Japanese bombed Pearl Harbor and all ships were prevented from leaving China. The Japanese placed Tom, his mother, and his sister in a concentration camp where they stayed for five years until the end of the war.

Only team to trade a player for a consultant's advice
Indiana Pacers, January 7, 1983
Jon Spoelstra earned a reputation as a marketing guru during 11 years as the Senior VP/General Manager of the Portland Trail Blazers. During his tenure with the team there was never a game that wasn't sold out. In 1983 his expertise helped Portland make the strangest trade in NBA history. Needing a point guard to fill a hole created by injury, Portland acquired veteran Don Buse from the Indiana Pacers. The compensation to the Pacers wasn't a player, but one week of Spoelstra's time as a management consultant.

Most dramatic reversal of fortune in a trade
Leroy Ellis and John Trapp, Los Angeles to Philadelphia, 1972
"Coach, say it ain't so." Players on good teams sometimes do
get traded to bad teams, but in the case of Ellis and Trapp
the transfer had the impact of falling off a 10-story building.
Early in the 1972–73 season, they were both dealt from the
NBA champion Los Angeles Lakers—who had compiled a
69–13 record in 1971–72, the best in NBA history—to the
Philadelphia 76ers, who would win nine games and lose 73,
the worst record in NBA history.

Worst display of gratitude after a trade
Scottie Pippen, Houston, 1999
Charles Barkley wanted to win badly, so badly that in
January 1999 he deferred part of his salary so the Rockets
could acquire veteran Scottie Pippen from the Chicago Bulls.
Unfortunately, the Rockets didn't prosper with Pippen,
exiting in the first round of the playoffs. After the season,
Pippen said Barkley didn't show him the desire to win and
made disparaging remarks about his "sorry fat butt." Three
days later, Houston put Pippen on a plane to Portland.

First Iron Curtain player to join the NBA
Georgi Glouchkov, Phoenix, 1985
In Phoenix it is remembered, but not fondly, as the
"Glouchkov Experiment." The Suns went deep behind the
Iron Curtain into that well-known basketball hotbed of Bul-
garia to land Glouchkov. The six-foot-eight, 235-pound re-
bound specialist had trouble adjusting to life in North
America. He spoke no English and Suns coach John MacLeod
complained that Bo Taklev, Glouchkov's translator, "was
hard of hearing so by the time I'd repeat what I needed him

to interpret for Georgi during a time-out, we'd have to go back on the floor." Whatever the problem—some believed it was an insatiable craving for American fast food—Glouchkov did not shine in the Valley of the Sun. When asked about his play the Bulgarian admitted it was sub-par, but noted that "I have done nothing for which I should be beaten or hanged." When Glouchkov arrived at the next year's training camp 25 pounds lighter than expected, the Suns cut him.

First woman to "play" in a men's pro league
Penny Ann Early, Kentucky Colonels (ABA), November 28, 1968
Early created news in Louisville in 1968 by becoming the nation's first licensed woman horse jockey. In a show of "male solidarity," the jockeys at Churchill Downs boycotted the first three races that she entered. The ABA's Kentucky Colonels responded by signing the five-foot-three, 110-pound Early to a basketball contract, even though she had never played the game in her life. Coach Gene Rhodes was not amused and protested to management. However, the Colonels owners not only kept Early on the roster, but ordered Rhodes to play her in a real game. The moment came on November 28, 1968, against the Los Angeles Stars. Early wore a miniskirt and a turtleneck sweater with No. 3 on the back (to represent the three boycotted races at Churchill Downs), and warmed up with the players and sat on the bench with the team. Early in the game, during a time-out, Rhodes reluctantly sent Early to the scorer's table, where she checked into the game. In the Kentucky backcourt she took the ball out of bounds and inbounded it to team-mate Bobby Rascoe. He quickly called a time-out and the

Colonels removed Early from the game to a standing ovation. Afterward she signed hundreds of autographs.

First player suspended for refusing to stand for the national anthem
Mahmoud Abdul-Rauf, Denver, March 12, 1996

Abdul-Rauf hadn't stood for the national anthem for most of the 1995–96 season, but with a month left in the schedule the NBA took a stand of its own. It suspended the Nuggets' leading scorer without pay until he complied with a league rule that requires players, coaches, and trainers to line up and stand in a dignified posture during the playing of the anthem. Abdul-Rauf, who was known as Chris Jackson before adopting the Islamic faith in 1991, said that his religious creed prevented him from recognizing the American flag and the national anthem as symbols of freedom. Instead, he claimed the anthem represented tyranny and a type of "nationalist ritualism" forbidden by his religion. Two days after being suspended, Abdul-Rauf changed his tune and agreed to stand. He said he would pray while the anthem was being played. "I'll offer a prayer, my own prayer, for those who are suffering. Muslim, Caucasian, African-American, Asian. That is what I cry out for."

Most Grateful Dead concerts attended by a Hall of Famer
More than 650: Bill Walton

Walton is a die-hard Deadhead. "They've been my life since I first saw them in the late sixties, when I was in high school," he admitted in one interview. "I attended lots of rock concerts when I was in high school and college, but after my first Dead show I realized that I had found a home." Walton numbers the Dead among the great teachers in his life and believes that lessons learned from the band served him well in the pursuit of his goals as a basketball player: "Their inspiration drove me. They taught me the importance of delivering peak performances on demand, and to always play with a sense of joy and creativity."

Longest piece of biblical scripture tattooed on a player's body
16 words: Larry Hughes
Hughes already had an impressive collection of 15 tats, including Silky Smooth, Boogie Down, Quiet Storm, Magician, and Grim Reaper, when he decided to expand his skin decor in the summer of 2000. At his favorite St. Louis tattoo parlor, Hughes asked his friend Nate to engrave all six verses of Psalm 23 across his torso from neck to navel. To save time and considerable pain, Nate suggested they simply highlight the most pertinent passage. Therefore, on his left upper arm Hughes now exhibits the words: "Though I Walk Through The Valley of The Shadow of Death, I Shall Fear No Man."

Largest height difference between two teammates
28 inches: Manute Bol and Muggsy Bogues, Washington, 1987–88
In 1985, the Bullets signed Manute Bol, a seven-foot-seven Dinka tribesman from Sudan, the tallest player to ever take the court in the NBA. Two years later the Bullets drafted five-foot-three Muggsy Bogues out of Wake Forest, the smallest player to play in the NBA. The Bol and Bogues carnival act lasted one season before both were shipped out in trades.

[2]

CASH
MONEY
MILLIONAIRES

The Los Angeles Lakers set a record for excess in 2000 when they had the words "Bling Bling" engraved in diamonds on their 14-carat gold championship rings. The hip-hop term for flashy jewelry and showy style was coined by the New Orleans rap family Cash Money Millionaires in the late 1990s.

First player to gross more annual revenue than a typical NBA team

Michael Jordan: Chicago, 1996

Jordan proved that one player can be bigger than a team—
at least in dollar figures. According to *Forbes* magazine,
Jordan's annual revenue from his salary and endorsements
in 1996 was close to the $100-million mark. At the time,
the average revenue per NBA team was about $90 million.

Richest long-term contract

$126 million: Kevin Garnett, Minnesota, 1997

In 1997 the Wolves flashed a six-year, $103-million contract
in front of Garnett, which at the time was the largest
contract ever offered to a pro athlete. Calling it an insult, the
21-year-old forward turned it down. A few months later,
the team rewarded Garnett's stubborness by upping the offer
to $126 million over six years. This time he signed. The deal
so horrified other NBA owners that it is credited with sparking the 1998 lockout. In October 2003 Garnett agreed to a
five-year, $100-million extension with Minnesota, bringing
his total haul to $226 million over 11 years.

Largest single-season salary

$33.14 million: Michael Jordan, Chicago, 1997–98

Some say he was still underpaid. This was the end of Jordan's
glory run in Chicago, but not the gravy train. No. 23 made
more millions after coming out of retirement in 2001 to play
for the Washington Wizards.

Most money to be earned by an NBA player by age 25

More than $200 million: LeBron James, Cleveland

James is a leaping gold mine. By the time he turns 25, the

muscular six-foot-eight, 240-pound swingman will have earned more than $200 million from playing basketball and from his assorted sponsorship deals for sneakers, trading cards, chewing gum, and soft drinks.

Most money earned per minute, one season
$100,000: Grant Hill, Orlando, 2000–01
Hill fractured his ankle during the 2000 playoffs, but that didn't stop him from breaking the bank later that summer. While recovering from surgery, Hill inked a seven-year, $93-million guaranteed contract with Detroit, the maximum allowable under the NBA's collective bargaining agreement. The Pistons then traded Hill to Orlando, which was salivating at the prospects of a team featuring Hill and Tracy McGrady, the club's other budget-busting off-season acquisition. But Hill's shattered ankle didn't heal. He played only four games and 133 minutes for Orlando in 2000–01, which means he made $100,000 per minute of court time. Hill's problematic foot limited him to only 14 games in 2001–02 and 29 games in 2002–03. All told, he collected $40 million for appearing in 47 games over the three seasons.

Fewest games started by a player with
a $100,000 contract, one season
3: Shawn Kemp, Portland, 2000–01
Kemp is a contender for the title of most overpaid NBA player of all time. Considered one of the NBA's brightest talents in the mid-1990s, the Reignman was a regular presence on TV highlight reels. But after leading Seattle to the 1996 finals, the six-foot-ten forward began missing practices and feuding with coach George Karl. Drugs and alcohol entered

the picture and his skills and dedication began to erode. By the time Kemp ended up in Portland 2000, the 30-year-old was a sad case. His weight had ballooned from 260 pounds to 317 and he was so out of shape that his teammates feared he might collapse and die on the court. But thanks to the $107-million, seven-year contract that he signed with Cleveland in 1997, Kemp was also filthy rich. Struggling with a cocaine habit, Kemp rode the bench for much of his two-year stay in Portland, starting only three games in 2000–01 and five games in 2001–02.

Only player to serve as his team's publicity director

Tom King, Detroit Falcons, 1946–47

In the NBA's first season each team's payroll was capped at $55,000, with most players earning between $4,000 and $5,000. Philadelphia Warriors scoring star Joe Fulks made $8,000, but his wage was dwarfed by bench-warmer Tom King, who earned a league high $16,500 for his combined duties as player, publicity director, and business manager of the Detroit Falcons.

First player to donate his entire season's salary to charity

Michael Jordan, Washington, 2001–02

At the Wizards' last home game of 2002–03, American Secretary of Defense Donald Rumsfeld presented Jordan with the flag that had been flown over the Pentagon on September 11, 2002, commemorating the one-year anniversary of the 9-11 terrorist attacks. Jordan received the flag in recognition of his financial support. He donated his entire 2001–02 salary, a reported $1 million, to agencies working with the families of victims in New York, Pennsylvania, and at the Pentagon.

Only draft pick to hold a secret auction for his services
Lew Alcindor, 1969

The Milwaukee Bucks won the right to select first in the 1969 draft in a coin toss with the Phoenix Suns. The choice was a no-brainer: UCLA's Lew Alcindor, soon to be known as Kareem Abdul-Jabbar, was clearly the best collegiate player. But signing Alcindor was not so simple. The ABA's New York Nets wanted the New York–born Alcindor badly, and they had the backing of the rest of the league, which felt that his drawing power would boost the ABA's popularity. Alcindor said he would play for the highest bidder and asked the Bucks and Nets to each submit one sealed contract bid. To ensure that the Nets had the highest bid, each of the ABA's teams agreed to pay a share of Alcindor's contract. That should have won the day, but Nets owner Art Brown inexplicably submitted a lower bid than what the league had agreed to. When Alcindor announced that the Bucks bid was higher, ABA officials rushed in with a counter offer, but Alcindor stuck to his word and signed with the Bucks. Milwaukee improved by 29 wins in its first season with Alcindor. Two years later, it won the title.

Most money lost by a player in bad investments
$18 million: Scottie Pippen

Considering that Pippen made more than $100 million in his NBA career he's not destitute, but even so, $18 million is some kind of kick in the head. Evidently, the former Chicago Bulls star lost the dough in shaky real estate dealings and investments in failing businesses. The extent of his losses became public when Pippen sued and won an $11.8-million judgment in 2004 against a Chicago financial adviser named

Robert Lunn with whom he entrusted $17.5 million of his money. And Pippen didn't pick Lunn himself. His lawyer made the referral. Pippen is now suing the lawyer and his law firm.

Most expensive clerical error

$4.1 million: Anthony Carter, Miami, June 2003
Gong! Carter's agent mistakenly failed to exercise a player option that would have enabled him to make $4.1 million with the Miami Heat in 2003–04. Carter was required to notify Miami by June 30, 2003, that he intended to invoke the player option on the final season of his three-year, $12-million contract. When the Heat received no such notification, the NBA listed Carter as a free agent. Carter's agent, Bill Duffy, claimed that one of his employees mishandled the situation. Carter, who had been averaging 4.1 points per game for Miami (the same number as the millions of dollars he would have received in salary), ended up signing with San Antonio for less than $1 million a year.

First player to successfully negotiate a contract by insulting his team's owner

Dennis Rodman, Chicago, July 1996
Coming off his fifth straight rebounding title and riding a wave of public adulation, Rodman brought a novel approach to bargaining on his new contract. The tattooed troublemaker began lashing out at Bulls owner Jerry Reinsdorf in newspaper interviews. "Offering me $5 million was an insult," Rodman told the *Chicago Sun-Times*. "And $6 million isn't much better. I'd rather quit than play for $6 million. If Reinsdorf would do the right thing, he would say, 'Let's pay the guy. He paid his dues.'" Did the tactic work?

Well, Rodman was later offered, and accepted, a $9-million deal to wreak havoc for the Bulls in 1996–97. Rodman summed up the negotiations by saying, "In this sport, they bring you in and use you and suck all the blood out of you and spit you out and say, 'O.K., who's next?'"

Fastest squandering of a $22-million contract

55 games: Roy Tarpley, Dallas, 1994–95

Tarpley is a poster child for wasted potential. The talented center was banned from the NBA in 1991 for nearly three full years for cocaine use, and the Mavericks, one of the worst teams of the 1990s, crumbled without him. Four years later, Tarpley was reinstated and Dallas gave him another chance, signing him to a six-year, $22-million contract. But only a couple of months after his return, Tarpley was banned again for drinking alcohol, which violated his aftercare agreement. Even after his NBA career ended Tarpley was trouble. In 1997 he was arrested on charges of burning his girlfriend's stomach with an iron, then he failed to show up for his court date.

Longest contract canceled after one season

15 years: Chris Webber, Golden State, 1994

In October 1993, a few months after leaving college, Webber signed a 15-year, $74-million deal with Golden State. But after just one season, Webber decided he didn't want to spend 15 years in the Bay Area. Citing a personality conflict with coach Don Nelson, he exercised an escape clause in his contract and became a restricted free agent. In November 1994, Golden State traded Webber to Washington in return for three future draft picks and Tom Gugliotta. Webber then signed a six-year, $58.5-million contract with the Wizards.

Largest contract for a player with multiple suspensions for drug abuse
$65 million: Lamar Odom, Miami, August 2003
The deal was $65 million for six years: big for anyone, but
the biggest to date for a player who had already served two
drug suspensions. Odom failed a pair of urine tests in 2001,
resulting in five- and eight-game suspensions, but that
didn't deter Miami GM Pat Riley. "We believe in Lamar,"
said Riley. The six-foot-ten forward lasted only one season
in Miami before being shipped out in a trade with the Lakers
for Shaquille O'Neal. The Lakers nearly nixed the deal
when they learned that Odom's agent had persuaded Miami
to insert a "trade kicker" in his contract. The clause guaranteed Odom a 15 percent annual increase in salary if he was
traded—which amounts to a tidy $7 million a year.

Largest contract for a player with a life-threatening disease
$22.6 million: Alonzo Mourning, New Jersey, July 2003
This situation had the potential to be a feel-good comeback
story, but that's not exactly how it turned out. Taking a
huge gamble, New Jersey signed Mourning to a four-year
$22.6-million guaranteed contract in July 2004, even
though he was suffering from serious kidney disease. Mourning played only 12 games in 2003–04 before retiring and
undergoing a kidney transplant. He made a remarkable
comeback with the Nets in 2004–05, but instead of being
grateful for the second chance, he poisoned the team atmos-
phere by criticizing management decisions and demanding
to be traded to a championship contender. Said Mourning,
"I stepped on the floor and it was like 'Wow, I don't care.'"
When he went on the injured list with knee tendonitis early
in December 2004, the Nets offered to buy out a portion of

the remaining $17 million on his contract, but Mourning refused because they were not offering enough dough. On December 17, 2004, the Nets traded the 35-year-old center to Toronto as part of a multiplayer deal for Vince Carter. Mourning refused to report. Although the Raptors could have simply made him sit out the rest of the season, they opted to buy out his contract for about $10 million. He then signed a $1.1 million deal, the veteran minimum, to join the first-place Miami Heat as a backup player.

Largest contract buyout
$30 million: Dikembe Mutombo, New Jersey, October 2003
The New Jersey Nets reached the NBA finals for the first time in franchise history in 2001–02, but were manhandled by gigantic Shaquille O'Neal and the Los Angeles Lakers. The Nets figured the solution was to acquire a big man. They swung a deal with Philadelphia to acquire the seven-foot-two Mutombo, a 36-year-old who had a four-year, $65-million contract. When the Nets realized their colossal error and cut the injury-dogged Mutombo loose prior to the start of the 2003–04 season, he still had two years and $37 million left on his deal. The Nets bit the bullet and forked over $30 million to free up some salary-cap money. The unwanted but enormously wealthy Mutombo then signed a two-year pact with the New York Knicks for $8.5 million a year.

Most money forfeited by a player in a contract buyout
$16.5 million: Shawn Kemp, Portland, September 2002
Kemp didn't fulfill expectations in Portland, as his play was hampered by cocaine and poor conditioning. In 2003–04, he had the sixth-highest salary in the NBA and he was a backup

player. Kemp was due to receive $21.5 million from the Trail Blazers in 2002–03 and $25 million in 2003–04. Unhappy with his part-time role, he agreed to let the club buy out his contract. Kemp reportedly ended up with about $30 million of the $46.5 million that the team owed him. He then signed a one-year, $1.03-million deal with Orlando.

Most money made by a coach in a buyout

$7 million: George Karl, Milwaukee, 2003

The Milwaukee Bucks thought so much of Karl's abilities that the club handed him a two-year, $14-million contract extension in March 2001 that made him the highest-paid coach in NBA history. To sweeten the deal, the team also sold Karl a one percent share in the franchise, which was worth $125 million at the time. But after the Bucks lost to New Jersey in the first round of the 2003 playoffs, management changed its mind and fired Karl, who still had one year and $7 million remaining on his contract.

Most money reportedly lost gambling on golf

$1.25 million: Michael Jordan, Chicago, 1991

And you thought Jordan was a bad baseball player. In June 1993 a San Diego businessman named Richard Esquinas published a book entitled *Michael & Me: Our Gambling Addiction... My Cry for Help!* In the book Esquinas claimed that during a 10-day period in 1991 Jordan had lost $1.25 million to him gambling on golf. No one believed his story until Esquinas produced the correspondence with Jordan and the canceled checks to back it. Early in 1992 Esquinas contacted Jordan several times asking him to pay off the bet. After a few token payments and many broken promises, Jordan agreed to settle the matter for $300,000. In March 1993 Jordan had a Chicago attorney send Esquinas $100,000. Then in May of that year, the attorney sent Esquinas another $100,000. But by then Esquinas had lost his patience waiting for his money and he published the book. Jordan later admitted to gambling and losing money to Esquinas, but denied the wagers were as large as Esquinas claimed.

Most money needed to feed a family for a year
More than $9 million: Latrell Sprewell, Minnesota, 2004
In October 2004 Sprewell, who was in the final season of a $62-million, five-year deal, claimed he was insulted by Minnesota's offer of a $27-million contract extension for three seasons. "I'm at risk here. I've got my family to feed," he said. The Sprewell clan must have astounding appetites. At $9 million per year, Sprewell, his wife, and his six kids could spend $8,000 for three squares a day for 365 days and still have enough money left over to cover a group membership to a Weight Watchers club.

Most money ordered paid to a convicted felon
$4.7 million: Vince Carter, Toronto, November 2004
Convicted felons may not be able to vote, but nothing can take away their right to sue. In November 2004 a U.S. federal jury ordered Carter to pay his imprisoned former agent, William "Tank" Black, $4.7 million in lost commissions and damages. Black was behind bars because he pleaded guilty to money laundering, fraud, and other charges for his role in a swindle that bilked millions of dollars from sports stars, including Carter, who lost $130,000. The jury ruled that Carter breached his contract with Black's company when the

Raptors guard dissolved the agreement in 2000. Black, who signed Carter after he left university in 1998, had sued his former client for $9 million in commissions for endorsement deals the former agent said he landed for Carter, as well as $5 million in damages. Carter countersued, demanding Black pay him the $15.9 million that Carter lost when Puma sued him over a failed shoe deal. The jury agreed that Black was negligent in handling the Puma contract, but decided Carter was not harmed financially by the negligence and awarded him no damages.

Most money sought from a player in a breach of contract case

$5 million: Michael Jordan, Washington, October 2002
Karla Knafel, a lounge singer, sued Jordan in 2002, claiming that he reneged on a promise to pay her $5 million in exchange for keeping their love affair a secret and not filing a paternity lawsuit against him when he believed that she was pregnant with his child. Although the child turned out not to be Jordan's, Knafel contended that he still had to live up to his agreement. In her suit she said that their affair, which began in 1989 shortly after Jordan was married, lasted three years. Knafle stated that Jordan told her not to worry about his marriage because he had a "business arrangement" with his wife, Juanita, that he considered Juanita "hired help," and that his agent, David Falk, advised him to marry Juanita to maintain his favorable public image. Jordan lost ground in the court of public opinion, but he won the legal battle. A judge threw out the lawsuit, saying the basketball star could not be forced to pay $5 million because such an agreement was legally unenforceable.

Smallest amount of money sought in a lawsuit

12 cents: Yao Ming, Houston, May 2003

It did not take Yao Ming long to learn about one American tradition—the lawsuit. In May 2003 the Rockets rookie sued Coca-Cola, accusing the soft-drink giant of using his image without permission on a line of commemorative Coke bottles sold in China that featured Yao and two other members of the Chinese national team. Yao asked for 1 yuan (12 cents) in token damages and an apology, citing "spiritual and economic losses." Yao's motivation for pursuing the suit was strictly business—the Chinese star had just signed an international endorsement deal with Pepsi. Initially, Coca-Cola insisted it could use the image of any player on the Chinese national team through an agreement with the management company which ran the team, but a week before the case went to court Coke issued an apology to Yao, ending the legal spat.

Most money demanded in an extortion of a rookie

$3 million: Carmelo Anthony, Denver, 2004

Police arrested three men in November 2004 for trying to extort $3 million from Denver Nuggets rookie Carmelo Anthony. Authorities said the men videotaped Anthony fighting at a Manhattan nightclub with a man known as Sugar Ray two months earlier. The fight broke out after Ray spat a drink on Anthony's girlfriend, MTV host La La Vasquez. (Ray and Vasquez had once been engaged to be married.) No one was hurt in the fight, but the three men demanded $3 million from Anthony in exchange for the tape. A meeting was set up on a New York City street corner using an undercover police detective posing as a representative for Anthony. A check was handed over and the three shakedown artists were arrested and charged with grand larceny and criminal possession of stolen property.

Most money lost for not reporting an injury

$250,000: Latrell Sprewell, New York, September 2002
Sprewell was fined by the Knicks for failing to report a broken hand he had suffered a couple of weeks before the team's 2002 training camp. The NBA collective bargaining agreement allows a team to fine or suspend a player for failing to report an injury, although it does not specify a maximum penalty. The penalty levied against Sprewell by the Knicks was the largest player fine in NBA history. The *New York Post* reported that Sprewell suffered the injury during a late-night party aboard his yacht. According to witnesses, Sprewell hit the wall while throwing a punch at a guest whose girlfriend had just vomited on his boat. Sprewell denied the newspaper's account and claimed he had actually hurt his hand skippering his yacht to safety during a storm. The Knicks guard filed a $40-million lawsuit against the *Post* for libel.

Most money paid in fines for technical fouls, one season

$20,500: Rasheed Wallace, Portland, 2001–02
Technical fouls are assessed for unsportsmanlike behavior, such as trash talking and cursing officials. Wallace's demented season in 2001–02 qualifies as the most obnoxious to date. The power forward was whistled for 41 technicals in 79 games. That broke his own record of 38 set the year before. At $500 per T, Wallace was out of pocket for $20,500. But that money was only the tip of the iceberg. If you include another $30,000 in fines for various other violations that Wallace was assessed during the season, plus the $280,000

he lost in salary for a two-game suspension, you arrive at the figure of $330,500—all lost for being a pain in the ass.

Most biblical fine

30 pieces of silver: Adrian Dantley, Utah, 1985–86
A contract dispute between Dantley and Jazz management during the 1985–86 season led to one of the stranger fines in NBA annals. Coach Frank Layden sent Dantley home during a road trip and fined him 30 pieces of silver (three dollars in dimes) for betrayal, a reference to Judas's selling of Jesus to the Romans.

First NBA owner to accumulate $1 million in fines

Mark Cuban, Dallas, 2002
Publicity hound, nutcase, or passionate fan? You be the judge. In his first two years as Mavericks owner, Cuban surpassed the million-dollar mark in fines. Most of the dot.com billionaire's fines were levied for his criticism of NBA refs, including one incident in which he staged an impromptu sit-down on the court in mid-game. There is no doubt that Cuban eats and breathes basketball. As he once said: "I spend every day thinking about the Mavericks. That includes time dreaming about the Mavs while sleeping."

Cheapest cost-cutting proposal by an NBA owner

Firing a trainer: Donald Sterling, San Diego Clippers, 1981
Sterling's reputation as a cheapskate is legendary. As Greg Cote of the *Miami Herald* once noted: "The limbo was invented when Donald Sterling first encountered a pay toilet." The Beverly Hills real estate tycoon has applied the same business formula to his basketball team that he used to

make a fortune in the housing market: buy cheap assets in rich neighborhoods, invest as little cash as possible into them, and hang on for the long haul. Since he bought the team in 1981, the Clippers have been a consistent doormat. But who cares about winning if your original $12.5 million investment is now worth $205 million? Sterling's miserly nature was evident during his first season as the Clippers owner when, in order to save a few dollars, he wanted to fire the assistant who tapes the players' ankles before games. He asked coach Paul Silas if he would do the job instead.

Most money collected from the NBA by a non-NBA team
More than $100 million: St. Louis Spirits, 1976 to 2005
Midway through the 1975–76 season, it became apparent that the NBA was considering a merger with the ABA, which had seven teams at the time. If the merger took place, ABA executives felt the NBA would take only six teams. Ozzie and Dan Silna, the owners of the St. Louis Spirits, and attorney Donald Schupak worked out compensation for the team that would not join the NBA. They proposed that the seventh team should receive a share of television money in perpetuity. As it turned out, the NBA accepted only four teams—the Indiana Pacers, the Denver Nuggets, the New York (now New Jersey) Nets, and the San Antonio Spurs—leaving three teams out in the cold. The debt-ridden Virginia Squires folded and the Kentucky Colonels owner, John Y. Brown, accepted a flat $3-million buyout. But the Spirits, who were not invited to join the NBA, refused a buyout, and so the four former ABA clubs agreed to give the three men $2.2 million, plus one-seventh of their annual television income in perpetuity. At the time, TV income wasn't a bonanza: for the en-

tire 1980s, the deal paid the Silnas and Schupak a relatively modest $8 million. But in the 1990s serious TV dough started rolling into the league, and every year a good chunk of it still goes straight into the bank accounts of the former owners of a team that never played a second in the NBA. By the time the NBA's TV deal expires in 2008, the Silnas and Schupak will have been compensated close to $200 million.

Most money spent per win by a team, one season
$3.16 million: New York Knicks, 2004–05

Welcome to the money pit. The Knicks spent an astronomic $104.4 million on player salaries in 2004–05 and still finished out of the playoffs with 33 wins and 49 losses. The four highest-paid players on New York's roster—Allan Houston ($17.5 million), Stephon Marbury ($14.6 million), Anfernee Hardaway ($14.6 million), and Tim Thomas ($13 million)—combined to make $59.7 million, which was more than the payrolls of 17 other NBA teams, including the defending champion Detroit Pistons. All told the Knicks shelled out $3.16 million per win in 2004–05. Yet as shocking as it sounds, this record for fiscal insanity could soon be surpassed—by the Knicks. The club is on the hook for $109.7 million in payroll in 2005–06 and has $86 million committed to nine players all the way to 2006-07. The lights in Manhattan may be bright, but the same can't be said of the Knicks' management, or the team's future.

Most money lost by a team, one season
$96 million: Portland Trail Blazers, 2002–03

The Blazers lost close to $100 million in 2002–03, believed to be the largest single-season deficit of any team in the history of American sport, according to a report in Street & Smith's *SportsBusiness Journal*. The team suffered $44 million in losses on its bloated payroll of $104 million because of a combination of factors. A national economic downturn hurt the club's business, as did a series of criminal acts and drug-related incidents involving Blazers players. As well, a decrease in television revenue for the first time in NBA history meant a smaller payout for each team. Finally, Portland also had to pay a penalty of $52 million in luxury taxes for exceeding the league's salary cap limit. Making matters worse, the high-salaried Blazers tanked in the playoffs, exiting in the first round.

Most money lost by a team for wearing baggy shorts, one month
$37,500: Minnesota Timberwolves, November 1997
The NBA wanted to see a little more leg. In November 1997 Minnesota was fined $25,000 and five of its players were fined $2,500 each by the league for wearing oversized shorts, penalties that the Players Association labeled "ridiculous." The fines were levied for failing to comply with NBA rules which state that shorts worn during a game must be no lower than one inch above the top of the knee.

[3]

NAMES

AND

NUMBERS

LeBron James holds the unofficial record for most nicknames compiled by a rookie. By the end of his first NBA season, 2003–04, the Cleveland Cavaliers phenom was known as "King," "LBJ," "Air Apparent," "the Chosen One," and "Bron-Bron." There may be more to come.

Longest player's name

48 letters: Dikembe Mutombo Mpolondo Mukamba
Jean Jacque Wamutombo

Mutombo's full name is nearly as long as he is tall. Just looking at it makes you dizzy. You have to wonder how they managed to fit all of it on his Congolese passport. The 48 letters are more than double the size of the seven-foot-two gargantuan's size-22 shoes.

Longest nickname for a slam dunk

21 words: Darryl Dawkins, Philadelphia, 1979

On November 13, 1979, in an NBA game against the Kansas City Kings, Dawkins rose high in the air, cocked his hands over his head and hit the basket with all the power his six-foot-eleven, 260-pound frame could muster. The result sounded like a bomb going off inside Kansas City's Memorial Auditorium. The backboard shattered and thousands of pieces of glass poured down on Dawkins and the Kings' Bill Robinzine. A chunk even lodged in Julius Erving's Afro. The basket counted and Dawkins dubbed the shot "The Chocolate Thunder-flying, Robinzine-crying, teeth-shaking, glass-breaking, rump-roasting, bun-toasting, wham-bam, glass-breaker-I-am jam!" Inspired by the enthusiastic reaction of fans to his power act, Dawkins began to baptize his dunks with inventive nicknames: "The In-Your-Face Disgrace," "The Spine-Chiller Supreme," "The Turbo Sexphonic Delight," and "The Get-Out-The-Wayin', Backboard Swayin', Game-Delayin', If-You-Ain't Groovin', You Best Get Movin' Dunk." None, however, exceeded the length or verbal grandiosity of his first creation.

Most nicknames for a player

More than half a dozen: Shaquille O'Neal

O'Neal's inventory of nicknames is ever-expanding, much like his waistline. The seven-foot-one, 340-pound center has been called "Shaq," "Shaq Daddy," "Shaq Fu," "Diesel," "the Big Aristotle," and "MDE" (for Most Dominant Ever). "The Big Aristotle" was a name that O'Neal gave himself after he won the 2000 MVP Award and quoted the Greek philosopher: "Excellence is not a singular act; it's a habit." Other monikers he has conferred on himself include "the Big Maravich," after he made nine straight free throws against Portland in the playoffs; "the Big Felon," after he made a game-saving steal against Orlando; and "the Big Cordially," because, as he said, "I'm nice." O'Neal has also invented handles for other players. Following a game with the Boston Celtics a few years ago, O'Neal was asked what he thought about Celtics forward Paul Pierce. "Paul Pierce is the fucking truth," O'Neal declared. The quote was published and the name—minus the expletive—stuck. Now, each time Pierce scores, Celtics fans chant "Truth!"

Most derogatory nicknames handed out by a broadcaster

Dozens: Johnny Most, Boston Celtics

The voice of the Boston Celtics for 37 years, Most was a self-proclaimed homer, someone who, as one referee stated, "could cause a riot at a High Mass" with his emotional, pro-Celtic descriptions. Most turned shoving matches into "bloodbaths" and minor fouls into "vicious muggings." Once, during a game in Detroit against the Pistons, he loudly declared, "Oh, the yellow, gutless way they do things here." Most frequently bestowed unflattering nicknames on

Boston's opponents. Kareem Abdul-Jabbar was "Kareem Puff," Dennis Rodman was "the Supreme Hot Dog," Isiah Thomas was "Little Lord Fauntleroy," and Washington's physical duo of Jeff Ruland and Rick Mahorn were "McFilthy and McNasty." As Boston's director of basketball operations Danny Ainge observed, "I always believed we had thirteen guys on the active roster—twelve wore uniforms and the thirteenth—Johnny Most—was high above courtside."

First player to have a rock band named after him
Mookie Blaylock, 1990
When Pearl Jam formed in Seattle in 1990, the band called itself Mookie Blaylock in homage to the New Jersey Nets point guard, whose NBA trading card was included with the band's first demo. Because of copyright and merchandising concerns, the name was later changed to Pearl Jam, a slang term for male ejaculate. But Eddie Vedder and the boys didn't totally forsake Mookie. Pearl Jam entitled its first album "Ten," in honor of his uniform number.

First team nicknamed after a hip-hop group
Golden State Warriors, "Run–TMC," 1990
In the early 1980s, the electronic boom-and-clank of rappers Run-DMC invaded the airwaves. Clad in gold chains, Kangols, and leather jackets, the three members of Run-DMC made both a musical and fashion statement. The name was later applied, with a slight twist, to Golden State's run-and-gun squads of the early 1990s, which featured explosive scoring from the trio of Tim Hardaway, Mitch Richmond, and Chris Mullin.

Only team to change its nickname because of an assassination

Washington, Bullets to Wizards, 1997

Although Washington's lone NBA title was won in 1978 under the name Bullets, when owner Abe Pollin moved the franchise to the MCI Center in 1997, he decided the team needed a new nickname. In his mind the term Bullets and its association with guns was too violent. According to Pollin, the impetus for the change was the 1995 assassination of Israel's Prime Minister Yitzhak Rabin. The name Wizards was selected in a fan contest.

Most contrived effort by a team to give a player a nickname

Houston Rockets, for Yao Ming, 2002

Sports teams often invite fans to invent a nickname for a mascot, but cooking up one for a player is something quite different—especially when that player hasn't played a game for the team yet. But that's exactly what happened after the Houston Rockets drafted Yao Ming in 2002. The club held a preseason contest to give the Shanghai giant a catchy moniker. The Rockets received thousands of suggestions, including "Ming the Merciless," "The Great Wall of China," "Ming Kong," and "Apocalypse Yao." Teammate Steve "Stevie Franchise" Francis started calling Yao "Dynasty," not in reference to the historical era, but rather because a "dynasty is even bigger than a franchise." Yet, despite all the efforts nothing has really stuck. Some reporters now call him "Chairman Yao," but the latest nickname to surface looks like it could be a winner: "Shaquie Chan."

Most inaccurate nickname for a player

Lafayette "Fat" Lever

A star point guard with the Denver Nuggets high-octane teams of the mid-1980s, Lever was never referred to as Lafayette. Instead, the native of Pine Bluff, Arkansas, was known by the unflattering moniker of "Fat." However Lever, who tipped the scales at six-foot-three and 175 pounds, was anything but overweight. The name "Fat" was given to him as child by a younger brother who couldn't pronounce his first name.

Most religious nickname for a player

Ray "Jesus" Allen

Allen's Seattle teammates often refer to him as "Jesus," not because of his miraculous basketball skills, but rather because it was the name of his character in the 1998 Spike Lee film *He Got Game.* In the movie Allen played the part of a flashy high-school hoopster named Jesus Shuttlesworth, who is pressured by his convict father (Denzel Washington) to attend the warden's favorite university in return for the promise of early parole.

Only basketball star named after a type of steak

Kobe Bryant

Bryant's papa, Joe, had a thing for food. He was nicknamed "Jellybean" when he played in the NBA in the late 1970s and early 1980s. Dad named his son after Japan's Kobe beef, the most expensive steak on the planet. Somehow it all makes sense.

Most appropriately named league leader

Larry Steele, Portland, 1973–74

For the first time in NBA history, steals and blocked shots were recorded as official statistics in 1973–74. The league leader in steals with 217 that year, with an average of 2.68 per game, was Trail Blazers guard Larry Steele.

First scoring champion nicknamed after a pimp

George "Iceberg Slim" Gervin

Gervin, who won three NBA scoring titles with San Antonio in the late 1970s and early 1980s, was given his nickname a few years earlier when he played for the ABA's Virginia Squires. Teammate Fatty Taylor dubbed the pipe-cleaner thin Gervin "Iceberg Slim," the street moniker of a slender pimp who had just written a best-selling autobiography about his life on the streets of Chicago. "That's the image I lived with my whole life," Gervin told one interviewer. "Big cars, a big hat. Live fast, die young. People in Detroit, the ones I hung out with, that's the way they lived." The name eventually evolved into "the Iceman," which referred more to Gervin's cool composure on the court than to his resemblance to a street hustler.

First player nicknamed after a serial killer

Andrew Toney, Philadelphia, 1980s

A lethal shooter, Toney was dubbed "the Boston Strangler" in the early 1980s because he kept killing the Celtics in the big games. The homicidal nickname took hold in the 1982 Eastern Conference finals when Toney torched the Celtics with games of 39, 30, and then 34 points in

Game 7 at Boston Garden as he led the Sixers to
a 120–106 win and a trip to the finals.

First player nicknamed after a cigar
Darko Milicic, Detroit, 2003–04
Here's a nickname with a historical connection. Red Auerbach, the legendary Celtics coach, introduced the concept
of the victory cigar in the 1950s by firing up a big stogie on
the bench in the waning minutes of Celtics blowouts. Milicic
was christened "the Human Victory Cigar" by Detroit
Pistons fans in 2003–04 because all his court appearances
came in the late stages of Detroit routs. The seven-foot
Serbian rookie averaged 4.7 minutes of garbage time per
game for the champion Pistons.

First player to legally adopt his nickname
Lloyd "World" B. Free, Golden State, 1982
The Brooklyn playground hoops star claimed that the nickname "World" was bestowed on him in high school because
of his 44-inch vertical leap and 360-degree dunks. He
changed it legally to World B. Free in 1982 when he played
for Golden State. The name had a message and Free delivered
it in characteristic showboat style through 13 NBA seasons,
placing second in scoring in 1978–79 and 1979–80.

First players to put their nicknames on their jerseys
Pete Maravich and Walt Bellamy, Atlanta, 1971–72
Score one for creativity and ego. Maravich and Bellamy broke
the uniform design code by adding their nicknames to their
jersey backs, complete with quote marks. Bellamy was
"Bells" and Maravich was "Pistol Pete."

Only player with a telephone area code tattooed on his chest
Jason Terry
One of the NBA's more eccentric players, Terry has several
superstitions. He used to sleep in his uniform before every
college game at Arizona. In the pro ranks, he continues to
follow other peculiar rituals, including eating chicken fingers
before games and wearing five pairs of socks on the court.
The point guard also has the number 206 tattooed on his
chest—the area code for his hometown of Seattle.

Most games played by a player after his number had been retired
405: Michael Jordan, March 19, 1995 to April 16, 2003
Jordan wore No. 23 because it was the closest he could get to
half of No. 45, the number worn by his older brother Larry.
In his first nine NBA seasons, he made 23 the most famous
number in the game. But when Jordan returned from his
17-month retirement in March 1995, he wore No. 45. Some
called it a calculated marketing move, designed to boost NBA
merchandise sales. Jordan wore No. 45 through the end of
the season and into the playoffs, when he switched back to
his old No. 23 during the Bulls semifinal series with
Orlando. The move didn't help the Bulls, who lost the series,
but MJ stuck with No. 23 for the rest of his career. No. 45
was actually the third jersey number worn by Jordan in the
NBA. He also wore No. 12 against Orlando on February 14,
1990, after his jersey was stolen from the locker room.

Most player names on one retired banner
5: Minneapolis Lakers
The Los Angeles Lakers have not retired the number of any
player from the early years of the franchise when it played in

Minneapolis, but on April 11, 2002, the club did honor five Minneapolis Hall of Famers—George Mikan, Jim Pollard, Slater Martin, Vern Mikkelsen, and Clyde Lovellette—with a banner. The banner also includes coach John Kundla's name.

Most numbers retired by one team
23: Boston Celtics
Well, yes the Celtics do have a glorious history, but 23 numbers is bordering on insanity. Not only have the Celtics retired more than twice as many numbers as any other NBA team, the total far exceeds the 14 numbers retired by baseball's New York Yankees, a team with a longer and even more celebrated past.

Strangest coincidence involving a retired number
Malik Sealy, No. 2, Minnesota Timberwolves
Sealy wore No. 21 for most of his NBA career, but when he joined the Minnesota Timberwolves in 1999, the six-foot-eight swingman switched to No. 2 because T-Wolves star Kevin Garnett wore No. 21. Ironically, Garnett had adopted No. 21 as a tribute to Sealy, whom he admired when he starred at St. John's University. Sealy's No. 2 was retired at Minnesota's home opener on November 4, 2000. It was the team's first home game since Sealy's death in a car accident six months earlier. He had been driving home from Garnett's 24th birthday party in Minneapolis when his SUV was hit head-on by a pickup truck traveling the wrong way on a divided highway.

First player to alternate numbers at home and road games
Rick Barry, Houston Rockets, 1978–79
Barry wanted to wear his familiar No. 24 after he was
traded to Houston in 1979, but because teammate Moses
Malone already had the number, he had to find an alterna-
tive. Barry compromised by wearing No. 2 at home and
No. 4 on the road.

First player to have his number retired twice by the same team
Bill Russell, Boston Celtics
Russell was a complicated and prickly character: he didn't
sign autographs and was uneasy with public adulation. The
Celtics had intended to retire Russell's No. 6 in a pre-game
ceremony, but when Russell refused to participate, the team
raised his number to the rafters in a private ceremony at
Boston Garden on March 12, 1972. Twenty-seven years later,
on May 26, 1999, a more mellow Russell allowed his No. 6
to be re-raised to the top of Boston's FleetCenter in a special
tribute hosted by comedian Bill Cosby. An estimated
12,000 fans attended.

Highest number worn by a scoring champion
No. 99: George Mikan, Minneapolis Lakers
Most everyone wore a number under 20 in the NBA's early
years, but not Mikan. Like latter-day superstars, the Clark
Kent lookalike wanted a number that set him apart. Long
before anyone had heard of Wayne Gretzky, Mikan picked
No. 99 and won three straight scoring titles while sporting
the double nines. No other Laker has ever worn the number,
but oddly the team has never retired it.

First player to refuse to have his number retired

Jim Loscutoff, No. 18, Boston Celtics

A hard-nosed forward who won five titles with the Celtics from 1956 to 1964, Loscutoff declined to have his jersey number retired so that a future Celtic player could wear it. Instead, a "LOSCY" banner was hung in Boston in his honor. The jersey number was in fact later used and then retired in honor of another Boston star: Dave Cowens.

Only NBA Hall of Famer inspired by a retired hockey number

Larry Bird, Boston Celtics

Legendary basketball star Larry Bird could be seen at every home game at Boston Garden standing isolated and staring up into the rafters while the national anthem played. In 1988 he explained what the ritual was all about. Bird said he was looking at the banner bearing Boston Bruins hockey star Bobby Orr's retired No. 4 for inspiration.

Most teams to retire one player's number

3: Wilt Chamberlain, No. 13, Los Angeles Lakers, Philadelphia 76ers, Golden State Warriors

The oddity here isn't the number of teams involved, but rather the number of years it took these teams to retire Chamberlain's number. The Lakers, Chamberlain's third and last NBA team, was actually the first to do it, retiring his No. 13 on November 9, 1983, 10 years after he quit the game. The 76ers waited until March 18, 1991, to retire his number, 23 years after he played his last game for the team. The Warriors, the team with which he recorded his famous 100-point game, did not see fit to honor Chamberlain's number until December 29, 1999, two months after his death, and 28 years after his entry into the Hall of Fame.

Only player who did not play in the NBA
to have his number retired by an NBA team

Wendell Ladner, New Jersey Nets, September 1975

Ladner's tenure with the Nets lasted less than two years, both
of them in the ABA, and he was not a star by any definition.
He was, however, much beloved for his personality and theatrics. A fiery competitor, the six-foot-five forward's main
role was providing protection for superstar Julius Erving. To
impress his fans, Ladner would often comb his hair during
time-outs and usually had a can of hair spray nearby. One of
the most popular promotions in ABA history was a poster of
Ladner posing wearing only his basketball shorts—a direct
takeoff of a similar shot of Burt Reynolds that appeared in
Cosmopolitan during that era. Ladner's No. 4 was retired
shortly after he died in a plane crash on June 24, 1975.

Only players to have two different numbers retired

Oscar Robertson, No. 14, Cincinnati Royals;
No. 1, Milwaukee Bucks
Julius Erving, No. 6, Philadelphia 76ers;
No. 32, New Jersey Nets

Hall of Famers don't often change numbers, but circumstances forced Robertson and Erving to make mid-career
switches. Robertson wore No. 14 when he starred for Cincinnati in the 1960s, but had to find a new digit after being
traded to Milwaukee in 1970 because shooting guard Jon
McGlocklin wore No. 14. This was the pair's second stint
as teammates—they also played together for the Royals in
the mid-1960s, where McGlocklin wore No. 11. Erving
gave up No. 32, which he had immortalized in New Jersey
and switched to No. 6 when he joined Philadelphia in 1976

because the number was about to be retired in honor of Billy Cunningham.

Highest number retired by a team
613: Red Holzman, New York Knicks, March 10, 1990
When teams want to retire a number in honor of a coach they have to get creative. New York chose 613 for Holzman because that represented his career total of regular-season wins with the Knicks. Not only did Holzman win more games than any other Knicks coach, he led the club to its only two NBA championships in 1970 and 1973.

Only team to retire the same number twice
New York Knicks, No. 15
Can a player's number be truly retired if it is retired again in honor of another player? The Knicks have no trouble with the concept. On March 1, 1986, the team retired Earl "the Pearl" Monroe's No. 15. Six years later, New York decided it should also confer the honor on 1950s point guard and former Knicks coach Dick McGuire, who wore No. 15 before Monroe. As a result, McGuire's No. 15 was retired on May 14, 1992, 35 years after he last played for the Knicks.

Fewest retired numbers by a franchise older than 35 years
0: Los Angeles Clippers
The Clippers have been a ghost ship for most of their existence. Through eight years in Buffalo, six in San Diego, and 21 and counting in Los Angeles, the Clippers have defined futility. Since moving to Los Angeles in 1984, they have had only one winning season, and that first retired number doesn't look any closer.

First team to retire a number in honor of its fans
Sacramento Kings, No. 6, 1986
In the Kings' second season in Sacramento after moving from
Kansas City, the club retired No. 6 in honor of its fans. Six
was chosen because it was supposed to represent the sixth
man, a non-starter who helps the team to victory. The bla-
tant PR move was later copied by the Charlotte Hornets who,
ironically, abandoned their fans when the franchise relocated
to New Orleans in 2002.

Most dubious collection of retired numbers
Portland Trail Blazers
As of 2005 the Blazers had retired nine numbers, second
most to the Boston Celtics. Nine numbers seems exorbitant
for a team that only came into existence in 1970 and that has
won just one NBA title. The Los Angeles Lakers, who have
been around since 1947 and have snagged 14 NBA titles,
have only put seven numbers on ice. Portland's honor role
includes such iffy characters as Dave Twardzik, Lloyd Neal,
and Geoff Petrie. Obviously that lone title is held in high
esteem in Portland: five players from the 1977 championship
squad, plus the coach, Jack Ramsay, have had numbers retired in their memory.

First NBA team to retire the number
of a player who never played for the team
New Orleans Hornets, Pete Maravich, No. 7, October 20, 2002
The Hornets' decision to retire Maravich's No. 7 during
halftime of the newly transplanted team's season opener in
2002–03 was pure PR. Maravich did star in New Orleans at
one time, but for a different franchise: the New Orleans Jazz.

Pistol Pete led the Jazz in scoring in four of the club's first five years before it moved to Utah in 1979. Maravich also attained godlike status by averaging an NCAA record 44.2 points per game during four seasons at Louisiana State in nearby Baton Rouge. "We're in New Orleans, and there's obviously only one name when you think of basketball in Louisiana and that's Pete Maravich," Hornets spokesman Harold Kaufman said. "So we think, with the NBA returning to New Orleans, it's a respectable and honorable thing to retire the number of a player who meant so much to the area."

Only team to retire its first number in honor of an opponent
Miami Heat, Michael Jordan, No. 23, April 11, 2003
A weird move, considering that all Jordan ever did for the Miami Heat was torment them, was made even weirder by the fact that it was the first number retired by the Heat. The jersey—half red for the Chicago Bulls and half blue for the Washington Wizards—was raised into the rafters at American Airlines Arena before Jordan's last game in Miami on April 11, 2003. Miami coach Pat Riley made the presentation at midcourt, stating, "In honor of your greatness and for all you've done for the game of basketball—and not just the NBA, but for all the fans around the world—we want to honor you tonight and hang your jersey, No. 23, from the rafters. No one will ever wear No. 23 again for the Miami Heat. You're the best." Jordan embraced Riley, waved to the crowd, and then went out and helped the Wizards beat the Heat 91–87.

[4]

HARDCOURT
SEX

Basketball bad boy Dennis Rodman
once remarked, "Fifty percent of life in
the NBA is sex. The other fifty percent
is money." In this chapter we delve into
record-breaking achievements in the
former category. Predictably, Rodman
and his libido figure prominently in
the discussion.

Most sexual partners claimed by a player

20,000: Wilt Chamberlain

Chamberlain's hoops career is studded with unbelievable numbers, so it's only fitting that his life off the court conformed to the theme. In his 1991 book *A View From Above,* Chamberlain stated that, since age 15, he had sexual encounters with 20,000 women, averaging 1.2 a day. That outrageous claim made him a lighting rod for critics and comics alike and prompted his longtime lawyer, Sy Goldberg, to offer an absurd explanation in defense of his client. Goldberg admitted that Chamberlain exaggerated his number of sexual partners, but that he did it for a good reason. "He was trying to say that it was better to be with one woman 1,000 times than to be with 1,000 women one time." This assertion, of course, was the opposite of Chamberlain's boast, which conveyed the impression that he enjoyed little, if any, repeat business. Of course, even sex addicts have to take days (and nights) off. So the Big Dipper made up for it at other times. In his book, he claimed that in one week while on vacation in Hawaii he bedded 30 women. At one birthday party there were 15 women, and Wilt. "I got all but one before the rising of the sun," he stated. "I wasn't able to enjoy the fifteenth birthday girl, but I did muster enough strength to sing her 'Happy Birthday.'"

Most celebrity sex partners claimed in one radio interview

3: Shaquille O'Neal, Los Angeles, April 2001

During the 2001 playoffs, O'Neal took time out to appear on a radio show with Los Angeles deejay Big Boy. In a segment called "Forbidden Questions," the Lakers center was asked to name a celebrity that he'd bedded. "Cindy Crawford," he blurted. When Big Boy expressed doubt, O'Neal repeated her name. Not satisfied to stop there, he added two more names: tennis star Venus Williams and pop singer Aaliyah. The loquacious Laker center finished up by ranking the love-making skills of his celebrity harem. "Definitely Aaliyah!" he said, rating supermodel Cindy as runner-up. All three women issued vehement denials, and a couple of weeks later O'Neal appeared on *Entertainment Tonight* to admit it was all a joke and that he'd written apologies to all three women.

Most NBA games played by a virgin

1,192: A.C. Green, 1986–87 to 2000–01

By NBA standards, Green's refusal to engage in sex may be the strangest kink of all. The God-fearing forward made it publicly known that he was a virgin and was resisting all temptations of the flesh until he married. Although this revelation made him a figure of curiosity and the butt of jokes (in 1999, *Sports Illustrated* dubbed Green "The Only NBA Player Who Has Never Scored"), he was not ashamed of his status, which he maintained throughout his 17-year career. "I'm proud to say that I am a virgin, and I don't hide the strength God has given me. You have to learn to respect yourself before you can start respecting other people." Maybe Green's abstinence gave him added strength—he played an NBA-record 1,192 consecutive games from November 19, 1986 to April 17, 2001. His virginity streak lasted even longer than his iron-man run. Green did not marry until April 20, 2002, at age 38.

Strangest relationship between a player and his wife

Doug and Jackie Christie

Repeatedly during NBA games, Christie raises his left fist
and extends his pinkie and index fingers toward the stands
of the arena. That's a gesture to his wife Jackie to let her
know that he loves her, and Christie once made it 62 times—
according to the count of Toronto sportswriters—during a
November 2001 Kings-Raptors game. Doug and Jackie have
a peculiar relationship. They get married every July 8, the
day on which they were originally wed in 1994. It's not simply a renewing of their vows: they have a complete wedding
with a preacher, guests, reception, and cake. When Jackie
attends Doug's games, he waits for her to come down from
the stands so they can walk off the court together. Jackie also
sends notes to Doug in the locker room and follows the team
bus in her car while talking to him on her cell phone. She
also forbids him to be interviewed by female broadcasters.
Jackie is so protective that when a fight between Christie
and the Lakers' Rick Fox erupted in a tunnel at the Staples
Center during a 2002 exhibition game, she rushed to her
husband's defense and began slugging Fox with her purse.
In January 2005 the pop music network VH-1 confirmed it
was holding discussions to make a reality TV show based
on the couple's odd marriage.

Nastiest sexual assault case involving a Hall of Famer

Calvin Murphy, 2004

Family dynamics don't get much uglier. The former Houston
Rockets guard was accused in 2004 of sexual assault by five
of his 10 daughters, who claimed that Murphy sexually
molested them between 1988 and 1991. After the charges

surfaced, the Hall of Famer was fired from his job as TV analyst for the Rockets. At the trial it was revealed that Murphy had 14 children with nine different women, of which he married only one. Murphy's lawyer argued that the true motivation behind the daughters' claims were resentment and money, specifically a fight over $52,408 in death benefits left to Murphy in a retirement account by their mother, who died in a 1996 car accident. The jury believed him. It took them just two hours to find Murphy not guilty on all charges.

First Hall of Famer featured in a sex tape
Julius Erving, January 2004

It was definitely not just what the doctor ordered. On January 27, 2004, an hour-long homemade movie of Dr. J getting intimate with an attractive brunette in a hotel room was delivered to a *New York Post* gossip columnist. The *Post* reported that the video showed a younger Erving in an "undershirt, boxers, and metal-framed glasses engaging with a voluptuous, dark-haired young woman with cinnamon skin, wearing a negligee." Dan Klores, a spokesman for Erving, claimed the video had been sent to the *Post* by Erving's former wife of 31 years, Turquoise, with whom the 53-year-old NBA legend was in the midst of a bitter divorce settlement. "This is a tape that was made 15 years ago, while Julius and his wife were separated," said Klores. "The decision by his wife's advisers to release it during their divorce negotiations is disappointing, especially since Mrs. Erving has had it in her possession for all these years." Turquoise's lawyer denied that she had supplied the *Post* with the tape.

First player forced to retire because he had HIV
Magic Johnson, November 7, 1991

In early November 1991, during a physical exam for an insurance policy, Johnson discovered that he was a carrier of HIV. The Los Angeles Lakers team physician advised him to quit basketball immediately in order to safeguard his threatened immune system. Johnson shared his discovery with his teammates, then held a press conference to announce that he was HIV-positive. The news stunned NBA fans, many of whom assumed that this meant Johnson was likely to die. The Lakers star contracted the virus through heterosexual sex. As he confessed, "After I arrived in L.A. in 1979, I did my best to accommodate as many women as I could—most of them through unprotected sex." Johnson would briefly return to the NBA two months later to play in the All-Star game, and then again to play 32 games in 1995–96, before retiring for good. Unlike many with HIV, Johnson has remained healthy. In 1997, his doctors announced that the AIDS virus in his body had been reduced to undetectable levels. They attributed this to potent disease-fighting drugs. Johnson's wife, Cookie, insisted that it was God's work.

First player to testify about engaging in sex acts at a strip club
Patrick Ewing, Orlando, July 23, 2001

Ewing was the first NBA player to testify in the trial of Gold Club owner Steve Kaplan and six others who were charged with profiting from prostitution, loan-sharking, fraud, and racketeering at the glitzy Atlanta strip club in the 1990s. The NBA veteran admitted on the witness stand that he had visited the nightspot about 10 times in the late 1990s and that on two occasions had sexual encounters with the female entertainers in the Gold Club's VIP rooms. Sexual favors were part of a marketing strategy to make the club a popular pit stop for pro athletes. "The girls danced and started fondling me," Ewing testified, recounting his first visit in 1996. "I got aroused. They performed oral sex." Ewing wasn't alone. Other NBA players who allegedly received sexual perks included John Starks, Reggie Miller, Antonio Davis, Jerry Stackhouse, Dikembe Mutombo, and Dennis Rodman. The trial ended when Kaplan struck a deal with prosecutors, pleading guilty to one count of racketeering and agreeing to pay a $5-million fine. He was sentenced to 18 months in prison.

Most extravagant complaint made by a player during his rape trial
Kobe Bryant, Los Angeles, 2004

We can get an inkling of the gigantic dimensions of Bryant's ego from the revelations in Phil Jackson's 2004 book *The Last Season.* The former Laker coach painted Bryant as a pampered star who took liberties to the extreme, caused dissension in the dressing room, and received more concessions than any other player he had coached. Among other things, Jackson noted that the Lakers had footed part of the bill for Bryant's travel back and forth between Los Angeles and Colorado for his court appearances in his ongoing rape trial, and yet Bryant still found cause for complaint. "Kobe was unhappy with the type of plane that was selected. He wanted one with a higher status." This nugget prompted Scott Ostler of the *San Francisco Chronicle* to note, "When you show up for your rape trial in a second-rate private jet, the message you're sending to the jury is clear: This is not a classy individual."

Most sex bites by a basketball announcer

More than a dozen: Marv Albert, February 1997

Who would have guessed that Albert was secretly a cross-dressing, flesh-eating sodomite? The broadcaster had called NBA games on NBC for 20 years without any notoriety, but that all changed when he went on trial in 1997, charged with sodomy and assault and battery. Albert's lover, Vanessa Perhach, accused him of throwing her on a hotel bed, viciously biting her back more than a dozen times, and forcing her to perform oral sex in a hotel room in Arlington, Virginia, on February 12, 1997. Perhach claimed that Albert was upset because she failed to bring another man into their bed for a session of three-way sex. She also said the 56-year-old wore white panties and a garter belt during the assault. Albert initially denied the charges, but his case suffered a setback when another witness, Patricia Masten, testified that Albert had attacked her while wearing panties and a garter belt in a Dallas hotel room in 1994. She claimed that he pushed her head toward his crotch and then bit her on the side of the neck. Masten said that as she tried to push the overheated broadcaster away, she grabbed his hairpiece and it lifted off his head—a truly ghastly image. The next day Albert cut a deal, pleading guilty to misdemeanor assault and battery in exchange for the dropping of the felony charge for sodomy. He was fired by NBC four hours later. In the aftermath, Albert jokes flooded the airwaves. For example: Why was Marv Albert happy that he was fired by NBC? Answer: Because the network gave him a pink slip. Yet, even more amazing than the tales of deviant sex was Albert's rapid rebound from disgrace. Just 16 months after his conviction, he was back on the air calling New York Knicks games for the MSG network, and five months after that he was re-hired by NBC.

First team to sign a registered sex offender
Portland Trail Blazers, August 2001

Why let a little detail like rape get in the way? Portland had no qualms about signing Ruben Patterson to a six-year, $33.8-million contract in 2001, only a couple of months after the Seattle SuperSonics guard entered a mod-ified guilty plea to a rape charge involving his children's 23-year-old nanny. Under his unorthodox plea, Patterson did not admit guilt but agreed that a jury might convict him. He also was placed on two years' probation and ordered to register as a sex offender. In the summer of 2003, with no hint of shame, Portland mounted a marketing campaign in which its play-ers, including Patterson, went door to door, courting fans with an invitation to a family night of basketball.

First pimp convention held during an NBA All-Star weekend
"The World's Famous Players Ball," Atlanta, 2003

There was a time when the NBA's mid-season break was about the league's all-stars facing off, but nowadays the parties, the celebrities, and the music are just as much a centerpiece of the weekend as actual basketball. During the 2003 NBA All-Star weekend in Atlanta, rapper Snoop Dogg and a man described by the *Atlanta Journal-Constitution* as "pimp-turned-preacher Bishop Don Juan" hosted "The World's Famous Players Ball," at Club Mirage. Atlanta officials were furious that a "pimp convention" was being held in their town, especially since they had just launched a crackdown on child pornography.

First former player to promote a sex product for women
Dennis Rodman, August 2004

Here's one from the hard-to-believe files. Beneficial Health Systems, a Salt Lake City company, announced in August 2004 that Rodman would be its corporate spokesman for a line of herbal sexual enhancers. "Dennis is a very unique individual," said Beneficial Health spokesman Phil Flynn. "He reaches a target demographic that we are extremely interested in with our sex-enhancement products." God knows what that demographic might be. Cross-dressers? Body-piercers? The lost and the damned? Beneficial Health's line includes EnduranceRx for men, a so-called libido-enhancer, available in pill form or as a taffy chew, and EnjoyRx, a sexual-enhancement spray for women. Rodman's agent, Darren Prince, declared his client an ideal spokesman for the products. "He's crossed over to pop star and sexual icon at the same time. This deal made a lot of sense."

Most pornographic ticket sales mix-up
Charlotte Bobcats, 2004

"What's your pleasure stranger?" Expansion teams usually make a few missteps, but the Bobcats took quite a tumble in their first ticket campaign. When fans dialed an NBA ticket number listed in a local phone book, instead of getting seats they were told to call a sex chat line. The correct number—800-4NBA-TIX—was established by the league in 2001 for tickets in any city, and it was listed correctly in the 2003 BellSouth White Pages, back when Charlotte had the Hornets. But the number in the 2004 BellSouth book, published in September, listed a toll-free number that referred callers to the sex line.

Age of oldest NBA owner involved in a sex scandal

70: Donald Sterling, Los Angles Clippers, 2003

The real-estate tycoon who owns the Los Angeles Clippers testified in 2003 that he regularly paid a Beverly Hills woman for sex, describing her as a $500-a-trick "freak" with whom he coupled "all over my building, in my bathroom, upstairs, in the corner, in the elevator." Sterling's graphic testimony came during a two-day pretrial deposition in connection with a lawsuit that he had filed against the woman, Alexandra Castro. In explicit detail, the 70-year-old recounted three years of transactions with Castro, whom he met in mid-1999. Although acknowledging that "maybe I morally did something wrong," the Clippers owner was not shy when it came to describing hour-long sessions with Castro, whom he credited with "sucking me all night long" and whose "best sex was better than words could express." Testifying that he was "quietly concealing it from the world," Sterling had a blunt appraisal of his relationship with Castro. "It was purely sex for money, money for sex, sex for money, money for sex."

First NBA owner tried on Court TV

George Shinn, Charlotte Hornets, December 1999

A self-made millionaire and ardent churchgoer, Shinn was the original majority owner of the expansion Hornets. When he brought the team to Charlotte in 1988, the town gave him a ticker-tape parade and the governors of North and South Carolina proclaimed the date of the Hornets' first NBA game, "George Shinn Day." Crowds flocked to the Charlotte Coliseum for eight seasons to see the team. But public perception of Shinn changed dramatically as a result of an incident on September 5, 1997. That morning, the Hornets owner picked up Leslie Price, a woman he had met while visiting a nephew at a drug rehabilitation center, and drove her to his home where she claimed that Shinn forced her to perform oral sex. Although police did not find enough evidence to proceed with criminal charges, Price filed a civil lawsuit against Shinn. Two years later, the case went to trial and was broadcast nationally on Court TV. Although Shinn was found not guilty, the lurid details that surfaced during the 11 days of testimony were damaging. Two former employees claimed Shinn had sexually harassed them and he admitted to extramarital affairs, including one with a member of the Hornets dance team. All this from a man who entitled his 1997 autobiography *Good Morning, Lord.* After the trial, Shinn's wife of 27 years divorced him. He then sold his house and moved to Florida, a move that angered many local fans who wondered why a man asking for a new taxpayer-financed arena wasn't paying taxes in Charlotte. Soon after the sellouts stopped. In 2002 Shinn, the hero turned heel, moved the franchise to New Orleans.

Most hush money allegedly shelled out to silence sex partners
$1 million: Shaquille O'Neal, Los Angeles, 2004
There was never any love lost between Kobe Bryant and Shaquille O'Neal. But nothing the feuding Laker superstars ever said in sports interviews was as inflammatory as the remarks Bryant made to police about O'Neal in July 2003 when he was questioned after a hotel concierge accused him of raping her in his room. "Bryant stated he should have done what Shaq does," a detective wrote in a confidential report obtained by the *Los Angeles Times.* "Bryant stated that

Shaq would pay his women not to say anything and already had paid up to one million dollars for situations like this." When Bryant's assertion became public, the married O'Neal angrily responded, "This whole situation is ridiculous. I never hang out with Kobe. I never hung around him. In the seven or eight years we were together [on the Lakers] we were never together. So how this guy can think he knows anything about me or my business is funny." O'Neal went on to add: "I'm not the one buying love. He's the one buying love." That jibe was a reference to the gifts—including a $4-million diamond ring—that Bryant lavished on his wife Vanessa after he admitted cheating on her.

Largest fine for transmitting a sexual disease

$592,000: Vernon Maxwell, San Antonio, 1998
In 1998 "Mad Max" was ordered to pay $592,000 in damages for knowingly transmitting genital herpes to a woman. State District Judge John Donovan granted a default judgment to plaintiff Sheila Rias after Maxwell continued to be a no-show in the case. The 30-year-old Spurs player was legally served notice of the lawsuit twice at his workplace—the Alamodome in San Antonio—but failed to respond or have an attorney represent him. Rias's attorney, Philip Bryant, presented evidence that his client contracted the disease from Maxwell in July 1995. Although Maxwell knew the high risks of transmitting his herpes, he still failed to take reasonable precautions or inform Rias of his condition, Bryant said. The court judgment included $200,000 in punitive damages for gross negligence. The remainder of the fine was to cover medical expenses, physical pain, and mental anguish. To avoid paying, Maxwell declared bankruptcy the day before the judgment.

**First player sued for sexual harrassment
as a result of a locker room incident**
Charles Barkley, Houston, October 1997
Lordy, Lordy. After a preseason game between Houston and
Phoenix, Elizabeth Anderson, a reporter for the Christian
Power, Health, Prosperity and Soul TV channel in Phoenix,
went to the locker room area to interview players about their
"Christian beliefs." After chatting with Rockets center Hakeem Olajuwon, Anderson was told by a security officer that
Charles Barkley would speak to her. She had asked to talk
with the Rockets forward after he was dressed, but when she
entered the locker room, Barkley was still wearing a towel
around his waist. Anderson decided to interview him anyway, which was not the wisest decision. Anderson later told
police officers that Barkley began to "wipe his private parts"
in front of her, and as the two continued to converse, he
removed his towel, exposing his genitals, then turned and
bent over, exposing his buttocks. Anderson told officers she
was shocked by the display. After the encounter she told
Barkley, "Charles, you need prayer." Anderson filed a sexual
harassment lawsuit against Barkley and his team in U.S.
District Court three days later, but the suit was eventually
dismissed. "It appears that Mr. Barkley did nothing more
than dress where the victim could see him," said Pima
County prosecutor Kevin Krejci. "She entered the men's
locker room voluntarily and knew it was a place where
men would be undressing."

First player charged with sexual assault as a result of a game incident
Dennis Rodman, San Antonio, 1996
There is no penalty for illegal use of the hands in basketball,
or at least there wasn't until Rodman invented one. In 1996

Dennis the Menace was sued for sexual assault by Lavon
Ankers, an usher at Salt Lake City's Delta Center. Ankers
claimed that the rebound specialist pinched her buttocks
after he dove into the stands for a loose ball during a playoff
game between San Antonio and Utah on May 6, 1994.
Ankers, who was seeking a hefty $750,000 in damages, came
out on the losing end of the decision. U.S. District Court
Judge David Sam dismissed the lawsuit, ruling that while
a pinch on the buttocks may have been insulting, it wasn't
"outrageous" and did not constitute battery.

Most sexual harrassment lawsuits filed against a player in 10 months
6: Dennis Rodman, 1998

Rodman's lawyer was one of the busiest attorneys in
America during a 10-month period between June 1998
and August 1999, Rodman, who may have been hitting the
sauce too hard, was served with six lawsuits from cocktail
waitresses and other women he had allegedly groped or
molested during nights on the town in Las Vegas.

First former NBA player convicted of unwanted touching
Dennis Rodman, 2001

Rodman broke new ground in the groping casebook in 2001
when he was ordered to pay $80,000 in damages to a Las
Vegas dealer who said that he endured unwanted touching
during a craps game at the Las Vegas Mirage Casino on October 12, 1997. James Brasich claimed he was humiliated when
Rodman rubbed dice at various times on his head, chest,
stomach, and genitals, while repeating, "Jack those dice off.
Jack those dice off." Rodman's lawyer, Randall Jones, argued
that Brasich did not believe Rodman intended to harm him,
but had merely rubbed the dice on his body for good luck,

and that the dealer consented to the touching by failing to tell Rodman to stop. The judge did not buy his argument. Brasich was not the only casino employee that Rodman laid his hands on that evening. Rey Novero, another dealer at the Mirage, said that a drunken Rodman also touched his genitals a couple of times the same night. "I didn't get offended," Novero testified. "That's why I didn't file a lawsuit."

First basketball MVP to pose nude in a magazine
Lauren Jackson, Seattle Storm (WNBA), 2002
Considered the most talented female hoopster to emerge from Australia, Jackson also owns the distinction of having 75,000 copies of her naked breasts publicly displayed in an Australian photo magazine called *Black+White*. In the spread, the 23-year-old WNBA MVP revealed everything except her down under. She appeared on the cover with the title "The Athens Dream," a tribute to the 2004 Summer Games in Greece. Jackson, who flew to Sydney to work with award-winning photographer Steve Lowe, was allowed to hand pick her photos. "I really did it with the Australians in mind," Jackson said. "It's a prestigious thing in Australia. Believe it or not, but my mom and dad loved it."

[5]

NOTHING

BUT

NET

The most outrageous NBA record of all may be Wilt Chamberlain's average of 50.4 points per game in 1961–62. No one has ever come within shouting distance of the mark. Just think: an entire team of Chamberlains would have scored an average of 252 points per game that season.

Only player to lead the NCAA, NBA, and ABA in scoring

Rick Barry

Here's a record that's safe for the ages. The master of the outside jump shot, Barry led the NCAA in scoring with a 37.4 points-per-game average for Miami in 1964–65. In his second NBA season in 1966–67, he paced the loop with a 35.6 average for San Francisco. After jumping to the Oakland Oaks of the ABA in 1968–69, Barry also led that now-defunct league with a 34.0 average.

**Most consecutive seasons leading
the NBA in points with a losing team**

3: Neil Johnston, Philadelphia, 1952–53, 1953–54, 1954–55

Only a select few players have led the NBA in scoring three times, but Johnston is unique: he managed to do it three consecutive seasons with a losing team. His first title in 1952–53 came with a Philadelphia Warriors club that posted a woeful 12–57 record. When the hook-shot artist copped his second crown the next season, Philadelphia was 29–43. When he won his third title, Philadelphia was 33–39. In 1955–56, Johnston finished third in scoring, but the Warriors went 45–27 and won the NBA championship.

Only player to lead the NBA in scoring and assists, one season

Nate "Tiny" Archibald, Kansas City, 1972–73

This record has legs. More than 30 years later, it's still hard to see how Archibald pulled it off. The six-foot-one guard led the NBA in both points per game—34.0—and in assists with an 11.4 average. Even more amazing is that he did this with a 36–46 Kansas City Kings team that played half its home games in Omaha, Nebraska. Archibald's nickname is the only tiny thing about the feat. Interestingly, if current NBA rules had applied in 1967–68, Oscar Robertson would share the distinction. The Cincinnati Royals guard led the circuit that year in assists with a 9.7 average and in points with a 29.2 average. However, the titles went to the player with the highest totals, and Roberston, who played only 62 games, ranked sixth in points and third in assists.

Only player to lead the NBA in scoring and personal fouls, one season
George Mikan, Minneapolis, 1949–50, 1950–51

Mikan was such a force that the New York Knicks once advertised a 1949 game at Madison Square Garden with the Lakers as "Geo. Mikan vs. Knicks." When Mikan walked into the locker room before the game he found his Lakers teammates sitting around in their street clothes. One of them greeted Mikan by saying, "They're advertising you're playing against the Knicks, so go play them. We'll wait here." Not only was Mikan a great scorer, he was also a hard-nosed physical player who led the NBA in personal fouls a record three times. In two of those seasons—1949–50 and 1950–51—he also led the league in scoring.

Only rookie to lead the NBA in scoring and not be voted Rookie of the Year
Elvin Hayes, San Diego, 1968–69

Few rookies have ever taken the NBA by storm as Hayes did in 1968–69. Unfortunately for him one of those rare rookies was Wes Unseld, who joined the big time the same year. Starring for the expansion San Diego Rockets, Hayes led the league in minutes played, field goals, and scoring average at 28.4, and logged 17.1 rebounds per game to boot. Unseld led in no statistical categories, but the Baltimore Bullets center had a major impact on his team. Baltimore improved by 21 wins and rose from last to first in the East. The voters rewarded Unseld by naming him Rookie of the Year and MVP.

Shortest player to win a scoring title
Allen Iverson, Philadelphia, 1998–99

At six feet and 165 pounds, Iverson may be small for a basketball player, but his ego makes up for it. "I believe in my heart I'm the best player in the world," said Iverson on January 15, 2002, after scoring a career-high 58 points against Houston. "I'm just a scorer. I try to put the ball in the basket for my team." In 1998–99, a season shortened to 50 games by the NBA lockout, Iverson was freed to shoot even more after 76ers coach Larry Brown moved him to shooting guard. He responded by winning his first scoring title, with a 26.8 average, and replaced six-foot-one Nate "Tiny" Archibald as the shortest NBA scoring champion.

Largest points lead in the scoring race
1,534 points: Wilt Chamberlain, Philadelphia, 1961–62

No, that's not a typo. Take a moment and try to wrap your head around the number. It doesn't seem real does it? The gap is so huge one could conclude that Chamberlain was playing in a different league, which in a sense he was. In 1961–62, Wilt the Stilt amassed 4,029 points for an unreal average of 50.4 points per game. The second-place finisher was Chicago's Walt Bellamy with 2,495 points. That total was the best of Bellamy's Hall of Fame career and the fifth-highest in NBA history at the time, yet he still trailed Chamberlain by a whopping 1,534 points.

Smallest winning margin in the scoring race

.07 points per game: George Gervin,
San Antonio, 1977–78

How's this for late-season drama? Entering the final day
of the 1977–78 season, Gervin led the league with a 26.8
average, with Denver's David Thompson second at 26.6.
In Thompson's last game, an afternoon contest against the
Detroit Pistons, he opened up with both barrels, scoring
32 points in the first quarter, an NBA record, and had 53 by
halftime. Thompson finished the game with 73 points, the
second highest total in history. The 73 points raised his scoring average to 27.15. Gervin, who played that night in New
Orleans against the Jazz, needed to score at least 58 points to
cop the scoring crown. The Iceman was fed the ball on just
about every play by his teammates and rarely passed up a
shot. He tallied 20 points in the first quarter, then broke
Thompson's record by draining 33 in the second quarter.
The Spurs guard quickly bagged six more points to give him
59, then headed to the bench, knowing the scoring title was
his. After a long rest, Gervin re-entered the game and ended
with 63 points. Gervin finished the season with an average
of 27.22 to Thompson's 27.15 in the closest scoring race in
NBA annals.

Most runner-up finishes in the scoring race, no wins, career

5: Karl Malone, 1985–86 to 2004–05

Malone's timing wasn't the best. If he had entered the NBA
either a few years earlier or a few years later, he would have
had a better shot at nabbing a scoring crown. But Malone
arrived just as Michael Jordan burst on the scene. The Mailman finished second to Jordan four straight times from

1988–89 to 1991–92, then again in 1996–97. He never won the title, even though Jordan's temporary retirement opened a window of opportunity in the mid-1990s.

Last white player to lead the NBA in scoring

Pete Maravich, New Orleans, 1976–77

This record is closing in on 30 years with no end in sight. Not even Larry Bird managed to do it. Maravich had a league-high 31.1 points-per-game average for the New Orleans Jazz in 1976–77. But even before that white scoring champions were in short supply. Since 1960, the only other white players to win scoring championships have been Jerry West and Rick Barry.

Highest percentage of a team's points, one season

40.2: Wilt Chamberlain, Philadelphia, 1961–62
37.8: Wilt Chamberlain, San Francisco, 1962–63
35.4: Michael Jordan, Chicago, 1986–87

These kinds of supernatural percentages will get you into the Hall of Fame, but they don't guarantee a championship. Chamberlain's Warriors didn't win the title in 1961–62 or 1962–63, and neither did Jordan's Bulls in 1986–87.

Highest points-per-game average by
a player while serving military duty, one season

38.3: Elgin Baylor, Los Angeles, 1961–62

Baylor was one of two NBA players called to active military duty after the Berlin crisis in 1961. (Lenny Wilkens was the other.) He spent half of the season stationed at Fort Lewis, Washington, playing only when he could obtain a weekend pass. He appeared in 48 games for the Lakers and when he did he was fresh, ready, and virtually unstoppable. Baylor's average of 38.3 points per game was second only to Wilt Chamberlain's mind-boggling 50.4.

Most points scored by a halftime musical entertainer, one game
26: Tony Lavelli, Boston, December 22, 1949
Lavelli could play—he set an NCAA career scoring record at Yale—but he loved to play the accordion even more. In his 13th game as a Celtic in 1949, Lavelli scored 26 points as Boston beat the Minneapolis Lakers. At halftime, Lavelli treated the 5,206 fans at Boston Garden to an accordion concert, one of about two dozen that he performed around the league that season. The NBA paid him $125 per concert. Lavelli was an accomplished accordionist, having once made a guest appearance with the New Haven Symphony Orchestra, and when he joined the New York Knicks in 1950–51, he studied at the Julliard School of Music. After two seasons in the NBA, Lavelli toured for three years with the Harlem Globetrotters, always providing the fans with halftime music on his squeeze box.

Most points scored by a player on his birthday, one game
61: Shaquille O'Neal, Los Angeles, March 6, 2000
On his 28th birthday, O'Neal netted 61 points and pulled down 23 rebounds against the Los Angeles Clippers. Prior to the game, the Clippers had denied O'Neal's request for some complimentary tickets. Following his monster performance O'Neal exclaimed, "Don't ever make me pay for tickets." For future reference: LeBron James was born on December 30.

Most points by a player in his first NBA game

43: Wilt Chamberlain, Philadelphia, October 24, 1959

Chamberlain had a knack of making a big impression in his debuts. In his first university game with Kansas in 1956, he set a new school record, scoring 52 points in an 87–69 win over Northwestern. He was almost as prolific in his NBA debut with the Philadelphia Warriors, pumping in 43 points and grabbing 28 rebounds against the New York Knicks.

Most points by a rookie, one game

58: Wilt Chamberlain, Philadelphia, January 25, 1960
58: Wilt Chamberlain, Philadelphia, February 21, 1960
57: Rick Barry, San Francisco, December 14, 1965

Chamberlain's record will be tough to break. Even he couldn't do it. Wilt the Stilt racked up 58 points (plus 42 rebounds) in a 127–117 win over Detroit on January 25, 1960, and then matched the mark a month later in a 129–122 victory over New York. Barry came within one point of the record in 1965 when the Warriors ace counted 57 points in a 141–137 loss to the Knicks.

Only player to score more points than his height in inches, one game

Wilt Chamberlain, Philadelphia, March 2, 1962

At seven-foot-one, Chamberlain was a tower of talent. But even he had to be amazed when he scored 100 points for the Warriors in a 169–147 win against the New York Knicks in 1962. After compiling 41 points in the first half, Chamberlain poured it on, scoring 28 in the third quarter and 31 in the fourth, even though the Knicks were double- and triple-teaming him. He stuffed in the final bucket with 46 seconds left. Since Chamberlain stood 85 inches high, the 100 points gave him a 1.18 points-per-inch average for the game. The only other player to come close to this milestone is 76-inch David Thompson, who scored 73 points for Denver in the last game of the 1977–78 season.

Highest percentage of a team's points, one game

83.0: George Mikan, Minneapolis, November 22, 1950
The NBA's first truly dominant big man, the six-foot-ten Mikan led the Lakers to five league titles in six years between 1948–49 and 1953–54. Opposition teams tried many different strategies to negate his impact. In this infamous November 1950 encounter, Fort Wayne played keep-away whenever it had possession of the ball. The result was the lowest-scoring game in NBA annals. Mikan notched 15 points— including all of his club's four field goals—in a 19–18 loss. Although a minuscule total, his 15 points accounted for 83 percent of the Lakers' offense.

Most consecutive points, one game

23: Michael Jordan, Chicago, April 16, 1987
22: Michael Jordan, Washington, December 31, 2001
Has there ever been a player who could light it up like Jordan? In a 1987 game against Atlanta he reeled off 23 consecutive points. The last bucket in the run made Jordan the first player since Wilt Chamberlain in 1963 to reach 3,000 points. He finished with 61 points—his third straight game of 50 points or more—but the Bulls lost 117–114. Amazingly, Jordan came within one point of tying his record 14 years later, at age 38, when he exploded for 22 straight in a Wizards' win over New Jersey.

Longest buzzer-beater in an NBA game

89 feet: Baron Davis, Charlotte, February 17, 2001

Davis is credited with making the longest shot in NBA history, an 89-footer with seven-tenths of a second left in the third quarter of a game against the Milwaukee Bucks on February 17, 2001. But Davis's amazing toss is not the longest in pro basketball history. Jerry Harkness of the ABA's Indiana Pacers hit a 92-footer at the final buzzer to beat the Dallas Chaparrals 119–118 on November 13, 1967. Since the ABA used the three-point shot, this was a court-length trey.

First player to lead his team in scoring without making a field goal, one game

Richard "Rip" Hamilton, Detroit, January 6, 2005

Hamilton pulled off this strange feat by hitting all 14 of his free throws, while going 0-for-10 from the field. His 14 points led all Detroit scorers in a 101–79 loss to the Memphis Grizzlies. The defending champions' anemic display prompted Pistons coach Larry Brown to exclaim: "I never thought I would have to coach effort. I've never had to do that in my entire life, and this is the last group I would have expected to have to do this with."

First player to score a wrong-way basket

Johnny Warren, Cleveland, December 9, 1970

The expansion Cavaliers set a new standard for stupidity in a game against Portland in 1970. Cleveland trailed 84–81 as the fourth quarter began. The Cavs won the tip and the ball went to Bobby Lewis, who spotted teammate Johnny Warren streaking down the court. Lewis hit Warren with a long pass and he went in to score the basket. Only one problem:

Warren had mistakenly stuffed the ball in Portland's basket and cost his club two points. "I thought I had a basket," a downcast Warren told reporters after the game. "When I heard the whistle, I thought I had been called for traveling or something." Portland's Leroy Ellis, who actually tried to block Warren's shot, was credited with the two points. "It's too bad Leroy didn't foul him and get a three-point play," joked Portland's coach Rolland Todd.

First player to intentionally shoot at the wrong basket
Ricky Davis, Cleveland, March 16, 2003
Cleveland led Utah by 25 points with six seconds in this 2003 game left when Davis took an inbounds pass and prepared to shoot at Utah's basket. Was he confused? No, simply a stats-obsessed jackass. Davis, who had 26 points, 12 assists and nine rebounds in the game, needed another rebound to post a triple-double. Utah's DeShawn Stevenson bear-hugged Davis before the attempt and was whistled for a foul. Davis made the two free throws to complete the game's scoring. "Let him try to get it when the game means something. I was proud of DeShawn and I would have knocked him down harder. They can put me in jail for saying that, but that's the way it is," said Jazz coach Jerry Sloan.

Most points, no rebounds, one game
54: Damon Stoudamire, Portland, January 14, 2005
Not only did Stoudamire not snare a single rebound in this 2005 game, he also had only one assist and one steal. Stoudamire asked for a copy of the score sheet after the game, not because it was such an oddity, but because it was the best scoring game of his career. The little guard set a team record

with 54 points as he shot 20-for-32 from the field and hit eight three-pointers and six free throws. Portland's other guard, Nick Van Exel, added 23 points, but the Blazers still lost 112–106 to New Orleans.

Most field goals attempted, no points, one game
17: Tim Hardaway, Golden State, December 27, 1991
A five-time All-Star who reached 5,000 points and 2,500 assists in the second-fastest time in NBA history (only Oscar Robertson did it faster), Hardaway was no scoring slouch. But against Minnesota on December 27, 1991, he could not find the bucket. Hardaway set a new NBA record by missing all 17 of his shots from the field. Despite Hardaway's loss of motor control, the Warriors won 106–102.

Lowest field-goal percentage by a league leader
.340: Bob Feerick, Washington, 1947–48
This figure reveals a lot about the accuracy of shooters in pro basketball's early years. Feerick, a guard with the Washington Capitols, hit an ice-cold 34 percent of his field-goal attempts and yet still led the league. In fact, only one NBA team—Baltimore—achieved a 30 percent success rate in 1947–48.

Most free throws made underhanded, career
3,818: Rick Barry, 1965–66 to 1979–80
It didn't look very stylish, nor very manly either. Instead of employing the standard set shot at the charity stripe, Barry used an underhanded toss, grabbing the ball around its sides, then bending his knees and bringing his arms and wrists forward in concert and releasing the ball in a high arc. This arc,

physicists have said, increases the chance of success, as does the backspin on the ball and the fact that the two-handed shot reduces drift left or right. Barry made efficient use of his limp-wristed technique, leading the NBA in free-throw percentage nine times. During his career, he made 3,818 free throws in 4,243 attempts, a 90 percent success rate. When he retired in 1980, it was the highest percentage in NBA history. Considering his incredible accuracy, you might think other players would have adopted the "granny" shot, but virtually no one else has copied it, not even Barry's four sons, all of whom played professionally, including three in the NBA.

Highest free-throw percentage by a face-patter, career
.877: Jeff Hornacek, 1986–87 to 1999–2000
Before taking a free throw, Hornacek would ritually rub his right cheek three times. Nervous tic? No, Hornacek claimed it was a symbolic greeting for his three children, who once asked him to wave to them at games. Hornacek said he couldn't do that, but offered a compromise. He told them he would pat the side of his face three times as a secret wave. Hornacek waved goodbye to the NBA in 1999–2000, posting a league-leading .950 free-throw percentage in his final season.

Most kisses blown at a basket, one season (including playoffs)
517: Jason Kidd, New Jersey, 2002–03
Kidd used to ritually blow a kiss at the basket before each of his free-throw attempts. It was meant as a loving gesture to his wife, Joumana, the same woman whom Kidd punched in the face in 2001. In that incident, Kidd was arrested on assault charges after Joumana called 911 and told the operator,

"There's just a bad history here. I told him this would be the last time, and he popped me right in the mouth." Asked later if she needed medical attention, Joumana said, "Don't worry about me. This is minor compared to what I usually go through." Kidd agreed to undergo six months of anger management counseling and the charges were dropped. Kidd recently stopped performing "the kiss," supposedly because his son TJ would imitate it during his youth games, causing a delay.

Most free throws missed, one season

578: Wilt Chamberlain, Philadelphia, 1967–68
Chamberlain's lone flaw was that he couldn't consistently sink free throws. He tried various approaches, including shooting underhanded and from the corner of the key, but nothing helped. As his career progressed, his accuracy actually got worse. In 1967–68, the Big Dipper missed 578 of his 932 shots from the stripe. Had Chamberlain made 151 more of those shots (an average of 51 percent), he would have led the league in scoring, rebounds, and assists—something no player has ever done. Wacky as it sounds, Chamberlain retired with a higher career field-goal percentage (.540) than free-throw percentage (.511).

Most free throws missed, one foul

5: Chris Dudley, Cleveland, January 29, 1989
During a 16-year NBA career, Dudley donated more than a million dollars to charity. However, the six-foot-eleven center had an aversion to accepting it for himself. One of the worst free-throw shooters of all time, Dudley showcased his appalling aim in spectacular fashion with Cleveland on

January 29, 1989, when he went to the line to shoot two foul shots. As usual, he missed both of them. But on the second attempt, Washington's Darrell Walker was whistled for a lane violation. Dudley was given another shot and missed again. But this time Washington's Dave Feitl was called for a lane violation. Dudley missed again. Amazingly, Feitl was called for another lane violation, and equally amazingly, Dudley tossed up another brick. As bad as this was, it may not have been Dudley's most inept display at the charity stripe. On April 14, 1990, with New Jersey, he missed 17 of 18 free throws against Indiana, including 13 straight, one of them an air ball.

Best three-point shooting percentage, career

.454: Steve Kerr, 1988–89 to 2002–03
Although he was not considered much of an athlete, Kerr had no equal in nailing three-pointers. The six-foot-three guard holds the first, third, and fifth best single-season NBA marks for three-point percentage, topped by his sizzling .524 percentage in 1994–95 with Chicago. Utilized mostly as a role player—and his role was hitting long-range jumpers— Kerr won five NBA titles in a 14-year career.

Most three-pointers by a player under indictment for rape, one game

12: Kobe Bryant, Los Angeles, January 7, 2003
One thing you must admit about Bryant, he isn't easily distracted. Despite having a felony sexual assault trial looming over his head, he hit for an NBA-record 12 three-pointers, including nine straight from downtown, in a 119–98 Lakers' win over Seattle on January 7, 2003. Declared Lakers coach Phil Jackson: "That was perhaps the greatest streak shooting I have ever seen in my life."

Most 50-point games, career

118: Wilt Chamberlain, 1959–60 to 1972–73

Chamberlain owns 15 of the top 20 single-game scoring totals in NBA history. In 1961–62 alone, he scored 50 points or more in 45 games, which is 14 more than Michael Jordan recorded in his entire career.

Most consecutive 50-point games

7: Wilt Chamberlain, Philadelphia,
December 16 to 29, 1961

Two days after Chamberlain had a consecutive streak of scoring at least 50 points stopped at five games (he was "held" to 43 points by the Syracuse Nationals), the Warriors center began a new blitz. He notched 50 against the Chicago Packers to start a record seven-game scoring tear of at least 50 points. If not for that "off" night against Syracuse, Chamberlain would have scored at least 50 points in 13 straight games.

Most points scored in a loss

78: Wilt Chamberlain, Philadelphia, December 8, 1961

This record says something about both the team that Chamberlain played for and the era in which he played. Philly was virtually a one-man show and offense was king. Despite his 78 points, Wilt the Stilt's Warriors lost to the Lakers 151–147 in triple overtime.

Most consecutive assist titles, career

9: John Stockton, 1984–85 to 2002–03

Standing a scrawny six-foot-one and 175 pounds, Stockton did not cut an impressive figure on the court. But few other players have had such an impressive career. The NBA's career leader in assists, Stockton reeled off nine straight assist titles with machine-like precision from 1987–88 to 1995–96. That broke the league record of eight, set more than 30 years earlier by another scrawny white guy named Bob Cousy.

Most consecutive games without an assist, career
99: Yinka Dare, 1994–95 to 1997–98
Dare came to symbolize the ineptitude of the New Jersey Nets in the late 1990s. The club wasted its first round pick (14th overall) and a bundle of cash on the seven-foot Nigerian center, who somehow managed to record only four assists in his four-year career and finished with more turnovers (96) than field goals (86). Dare stumbled around the court for 99 consecutive games before posting his first assist.

Only player to average a triple-double, one season
Oscar Robertson, Cincinnati, 1961–62
In only his second NBA season, Robertson set a record which ranks as one of the greatest individual achievements in basketball or any other sport. The Big O averaged a triple-double for the entire 1961–62 season: 30.8 points, 11.4 assists, and 12.5 rebounds per game. More than half his games (41 of 79) were triple-doubles, and seven times he topped 15 assists and 15 rebounds in the same game. Those 41 triple-double games represent the NBA single-season record.

Only player to record a double triple-double, one game
Wilt Chamberlain, Philadelphia, February 2, 1968
This feat is so rare that few people have even heard of a double triple-double (at least 20 of any three statistics).

On Ground Hog Day in 1968, Chamberlain compiled a jaw-dropping 22 points, 25 rebounds, and 21 assists in a 131–121 victory over Detroit.

Most tainted triple-double

Anthony Bowie, Orlando, March 19, 1996

Subbing for injured Nick Anderson, Bowie found himself with 20 points, 10 rebounds, and nine assists with four seconds left on the clock and his Magic leading Detroit by 20 points. Desperately wanting his first triple-double, Bowie called time-out. On the ensuing play, he tossed an inbounds lob to teammate David Vaughn, who scored, while the peeved Pistons stood watching with their hands on their hips. "Who knows when this opportunity might come along again?" Bowie said in his defense. "Just because I called a time-out doesn't make me a bad guy." Well, actually it does. The Pistons were fined by the NBA for their lack of effort on the play.

Most combined points by two opposing players, one game

141: Wilt Chamberlain (78), San Francisco and Elgin Baylor (63), Los Angeles, December 8, 1961

It was a classic West Coast shootout. Chamberlain won the individual duel with 78 points, breaking Baylor's single-game NBA record of 71 points, but Baylor's team won the game, 151 to 147 in triple overtime, as he poured in 63. The pair's combined total of 141 points was two more than the total amassed in Chamberlain's legendary 100-point game later that season, in which Richie Guerin of the Knicks scored 39.

[6]

THE
FANS
GO WILD

Which NBA team has the loudest fans? Sacramento claims it does. In an attempt to set a world record, the cowbell-wielding throng at Arco Arena produced 112 decibels of noise, the equivalent of a jet engine, before a playoff game against the Lakers on May 18, 2002.

First NBA team to draw one million fans, one season

Detroit Pistons, 1987–88

Experts in the art of thuggery, Detroit's "Bad Boys" may not have been popular in 23 NBA cities, but they were a hot commodity in Motown. The team drew 1,066,605 fans in 1987–88 as it led the Eastern Conference in wins and advanced to the NBA finals before losing to the Lakers. The next year Detroit took the title, yet drew 190,000 fewer fans. The decline wasn't due to a drop in popularity: the Pistons had moved from the huge Pontiac Silverdome to the 21,000-seat Palace of Auburn Hills, which the club sold out for five straight years.

Largest single-season increase in attendance caused by a rookie

6,791 fans per game: LeBron James, Cleveland, 2003–04

Cleveland drew 11,496 fans per game in 2002–03, the second worst in the NBA. The next year, average home attendance rose to 18,287, a jump of 6,791 per game. The increase was due entirely to the arrival of rookie sensation LeBron James. Not only did Cleveland sell out 16 home games, including 10 of its last 14 at Gund Arena, the club also sold out 33 of 41 games on the road. Even more remarkable, the Cavs jumped from 27th of 29 teams in road attendance to second behind only the Los Angeles Lakers. James's economic impact was immediate. According to *Forbes* magazine, the value of Cleveland's franchise surged by more than $35 million.

Largest NBA attendance, one game

62,046: Atlanta vs. Chicago, Georgia Dome, March 27, 1998

Michael Jordan could draw a crowd, both on the court and in
the stands. The lure of seeing His Airness in what many felt
might be his last game in Atlanta drew a record 62,046 fans
to the Georgia Dome for a clash with the Bulls. Demand was
so intense that 5,000 of the seats sold were dubbed "screen
only," meaning that they offered no direct view of the game.
Instead, those fans had to watch the action on the stadium's
giant video screens.

Smallest attendance for a pro game

*89: Houston vs. New York (ABA), Sam Houston Coliseum,
April 2, 1969*

Gauging true attendance is always a tricky thing, as teams
routinely pad the figures. But no amount of padding could
conceal the acres of empty seats at Sam Houston Coliseum
during the Houston Mavericks' second and last ABA season.
In February and March 1969, the Mavs drew an official average of 355 spectators per game. At their final home game,
only 89 fans showed up. They saw Houston post a franchise
record for points in a 149–132 win over the New York Nets.

Most consecutive home sellouts

814: Portland Trail Blazers, 1977 to 1995

Blazermania bloomed in April 1977 when Portland qualified
for the playoffs for the first time in its seven-year existence
and then made a Cinderella run to take the NBA championship. The sellout streak ended after the Trail Blazers were
swept in back-to-back seasons in the first round of the
playoffs: by San Antonio in 1993 and by Houston in 1994.

Most people killed in a championship victory celebration

7: Detroit, June 14, 1990

When the Pistons won the NBA title in 1990, fans took to the streets to celebrate. But the party soon turned violent. By the time it was over seven people were killed and hundreds were injured by gunfire, stabbings, and fighting. Looting and raucous behavior led to 65 arrests and thousands of dollars of property damage.

First NBA fan promotion

Toronto vs. New York, November 1, 1946

Contrary to what many suppose, the first NBA game was played not in the U.S., but rather in Canada at Toronto's Maple Leaf Gardens, as the hometown Huskies hosted the Knicks. With the Toronto Maple Leafs' hockey image to contend with and only one Canadian player on its roster, the Huskies tried hard to promote the game. The club ran large newspaper ads bearing a photo of six-foot-eight center George Nostrand, Toronto's tallest player, that asked, "Can You Top This?" Any fan taller than Nostrand was granted free admission to the season opener. The contest drew 7,090, a good crowd considering that pro basketball was an unproven commodity.

Most rats thrown at an NBA team, one week

2: Philadelphia 76ers, January 2003

In the final minute of a game between the visiting 76ers and the Phoenix Suns on January 2, 2003, a live rat was thrown onto the America West Arena court. It hit the floor and lay twitching on the baseline until it was swept away. Making the incident doubly odd, it was the second rodent hurled on the court at a Sixers game in a week. Five days before in Utah, a rat was launched from the upper section of the arena during the second quarter. "They seem to be following us, I guess," noted 76ers point guard Eric Snow. "I don't know why. I hope they don't start a trend. They need to stop it because they're throwing them up so high, somebody's going to get hit and somebody's going to get hurt."

Most successful Elvis impersonator promotion at an NBA game
Buffalo Braves, April 8, 1978
The Braves were headed for extinction in 1977–78 with a lousy team and listless attendance. But the club did manage to sell out its last home game by staging a novel promotion. The Braves sold a sponsorship to the local Budweiser distributorship and hired an Elvis impersonator to perform not long after the death of Elvis. It was billed as "The King of Beers presents: A salute to the King of Rock and Roll and the Buffalo Braves." Attendance, normally around 4,000, filled 19,000-seat Memorial Auditorium to the rafters to watch the Braves lose 118–107 to the Knicks. It was Buffalo's last sellout: next season the franchise moved to San Diego.

Most wig-wearing fans at an NBA game
6,213: Detroit, Palace of the Auburn Hills, March 19, 2004
In a drive to set a world record, the Pistons organized a "Spirit Wig Night." The club handed out 5,000 red-white-and-blue wigs, styled to resemble center Ben Wallace's bushy Afro, to kids 14 years and younger. Other fans were encouraged to don hairpieces to set a new Guinness World Record for most wigs worn to a sporting event. The previous mark of 5,574 was set at a rugby game in Australia in 2003. Not only did Pistons

fans establish a new record for artificial hair, they also saw their team whip the visiting Denver Nuggets 94–75.

Largest owner fine caused by a Mexican food promotion
$10,000: Mark Cuban, Dallas, February 2001

A fight broke out at the end of a February 15, 2001, game between Dallas and Cleveland when the Mavericks tried to reach 100 points in a blowout victory so fans could get coupons for 99-cent chalupas as part of a Taco Bell promotion. Fans began chanting "Cha-lu-pas! Cha-lu-pas!"as the clock wound down and the Mavs neared the 100-point mark, setting the stage for the ugliness that followed. The Cavaliers were still upset after the game. "It's bigger than chalupas," said Wesley Person, who drilled Dallas's Gary Trent after Trent launched the late jumper that put Dallas over 100. "Their coach called a play with 10 seconds left in a 20-point game. That's disrespect." When the melee started, Mavericks owner Mark Cuban rushed onto the court in what he claimed was a bid to aid his players. For this infraction he was fined $10,000—enough to buy 10,101 chalupas—and was banned from Reunion Arena for two games. Cuban later apologized to the Cavaliers, who feature the same fast-food promotion.

First NBA team to award a fan a championship ring
Detroit Pistons, November 2, 2004

It's no play on words. Dave Muehring, a 50-year-old Detroit firefighter, was the lucky winner of a random draw for a $15,000 Detroit Pistons' championship ring. Muehring was presented with his prize before Detroit's season-opener against Houston as players and coaches raised a banner celebrating their 2004 NBA title and received their rings.

The team made the gesture as a thank you to the fans who supported the club during its drive to the championship. Muehring, whose name was plucked from a bin containing 25,000 entries, admitted that he attended only four Pistons games in 2003–04, but said that he was a season ticket holder of the NHL's Detroit Red Wings.

First bobblehead doll giveaway that required an armed escort
LeBron James, Cleveland, March 1, 2004
Well, "required" may be pushing it. There was more than a bit of show business involved in the first LeBron James bobblehead promotion night. The 10,000 nodding dolls arrived at Cleveland's Gund Arena accompanied by an armored truck, gun-toting guards, news helicopters, reporters, and the team's mascot, Moondog. The frenzy only increased two days later as fans began lining up outside the arena hours before game time in order to get their hands on one of the seven-inch figurines, causing a rush-hour traffic jam.

Largest fine for spitting on a fan
$10,000: Charles Barkley, Philadelphia, March 1990
After listening to a New Jersey fan hurl insults at a 1990 game, Barkley finally lost his cool and turned around and spat at the heckler. Bad move. The wad of phlegm missed his intended target and hit an eight-year-old girl. Barkley said later that he felt bad about hitting the child and did go out of his way to make it up to her family, but the NBA gave him a $10,000 fine. Many felt that the incident cost Barkley the Most Valuable Player award that year, which went to Magic Johnson in a close vote. Barkley refused to apologize for spitting at the heckler, stating, "The guy is lucky to be alive."

Longest player suspension caused by flying beer

72 games: Ron Artest, Indiana, November 2004

Another evening of wonderful family entertainment. There was less than a minute left in a game on November 19, 2004, between the Pacers and Pistons when Detroit's Ben Wallace responded to a foul by shoving Indiana's Ron Artest. The Pacers forward retreated to the scorer's table and lay atop it, hands behind his head in a mocking manner. But when a Detroit fan hit Artest with a cup of beer, he suddenly woke up and stormed into the stands, throwing punches as he climbed over seats. Teammate Stephen Jackson quickly joined the fray and started tossing punches too. The fight continued for several minutes with Artest and Jermaine O'Neal uncorking haymakers at another fan near the Detroit bench. When Indiana's players and coaches finally left the floor they were showered with beer, popcorn, and assorted debris, including a folding chair. Nine players were suspended for a total of 143 games. Artest received the harshest punishment: he was exiled for the remaining 72 games of the season.

Most famous verbal exchange between a celebrity fan and a player

Spike Lee and Reggie Miller, New York vs. Indiana, June 1, 1994

Film directors are supposed to have a sense of the dramatic, so it is only fitting that Lee should get credit for sparking one of the most stirring playoff performances at Madison Square Garden. In Game 5 of the 1994 Eastern Conference finals, the Knicks nebbish began razzing Indiana's Reggie Miller, who had been having an off-night, and ended up in a trash-talking duel that lasted the entire game. Lee's verbal volleys only fired Miller up. He scored 25 points in the fourth quarter, including five treys (an NBA playoff record for one quarter), to spark the Pacers to a 93–86 victory. Lee was saved from permanent Knicks purgatory when New York rallied to win the last two games of the series.

Most NBA player impersonations by a fan
2: Barry Bremen, 1979 and 1981

Bremen began his strange career as sports impostor by donning a Kansas City Kings uniform, slipping onto the court during pre-game warm-ups at the Pontiac Silverdome prior to the 1979 NBA All-Star game, and shooting layups with the other players. The Michigan salesman repeated his act in a Houston Rockets uniform at the 1981 All-Star game at the Coliseum in Richfield, Ohio. Other Bremen stunts included playing nine practice holes at the 1979 U.S. Open, shagging fly balls with outfielder Fred Lynn prior to the 1981 Major League All-Star game, and suiting up with the NFC All-Stars at the 1980 NFL Pro Bowl. Bremen was less successful when he tried to dance with the Dallas Cowboys cheerleaders at a Cowboys-Redskins game. He prepared for the occasion by shaving his legs and having a cheerleader outfit custom-made. As the game began, Bremen burst onto the sidelines wearing white vinyl boots, hot pants, a blond wig, and a halter top over a padded bra. He got out only one "Go Dallas!" before security guards hauled him away

Most infamous heckler
Robin Ficker, Washington, 1984–85 to 1996–97

The Bethesda lawyer was a fixture at Washington Bullets games for 12 years, often clad in a homemade Bullets T-shirt and always berating opposing players from his seat in the front row. Ficker would try to distract the opposing team by reading aloud from books or newspapers, holding up rubber chickens or shouting at players through a megaphone as they huddled with their coaches. *The Sporting News* called him the "most obnoxious, most embarrassing fan in America." Utah Jazz coach Frank Layden once tried to attack Ficker and the Golden State Warriors dumped a bucket of Gatorade on his head. The Bullets had a love-hate relationship with Ficker, whose monologues often psyched out the opposing team but also annoyed fans who sat near him. Even so, he had his supporters. Charles Barkley of the Phoenix Suns paid Ficker's travel expenses to sit behind the Chicago Bulls bench during a playoff game against Phoenix in 1993. After the NBA created a rule prohibiting fans from engaging in verbal abuse that interferes with communication between coaches and players, Ficker canceled his season tickets.

Most famous fan to expose his buttocks at a game
Jack Nicholson, Boston vs. Los Angeles, June 12, 1984
With his designer sunglasses and his courtside seat, Nicholson has long been an institution at Lakers home games. The actor is such a serious fan that movie producers have had to organize their shooting schedules to allow him to attend Lakers games. His most memorable basketball cameo occurred during Game 7 of the 1984 NBA finals between the Lakers and the Celtics. That night, Nicholson began taunting the Boston Garden fans from the safety of his private box. At one point, he put his hand around his throat, suggesting that Boston was about to choke. To Nicholson's chagrin, however, the Celtics took the lead—and held it. With the clock running down and his beloved Lakers about

to lose, Nicholson vented his frustration by dropping his pants and mooning the crowd. Age has not dimmed Nicholson's fanaticism. During a May 12, 2003, playoff game against San Antonio, the 67-year-old actor became so incensed by a foul called on Shaquille O'Neal that he stepped onto the court at the Staples Center and began screaming insults at the referee. Ironically, at the time of this outburst, Nicholson was starring in a movie in which he played the role of an anger-management therapist.

First celebrity basketball fan to cause the creation of a law
Calvin Klein, 2004
Fashion trendsetter Calvin Klein was the inspiration for a new law passed by New York City in 2004 aimed at keeping rowdy fans away from athletes. Anyone found guilty under the "Calvin Klein bill" now faces a fine of $25,000 and a year in jail. The incident in question took place at a Knicks-Raptors game on March 25, 2003. With 2:11 remaining in the fourth quarter, Klein got up from his courtside seat and approached Knicks guard Latrell Sprewell as he was about to throw an inbounds pass. The fashion designer grabbed Sprewell by the arm and said a few words before being ushered back to his seat by Garden security. Sprewell later admitted that Klein was "trying to say something, but he was just mumbling." Two weeks later, Klein checked into a clinic for substance-abuse treatment.

Most money bid for an NBA ticket in an Internet auction
$101,300: October 2001
New York Knicks celebrity fan Spike Lee sold one of his two courtside tickets to Michael Jordan's comeback game on

October 30, 2001, for $101,300 on an Internet auction. Lee donated the money to the Widows and Children's Fund set up by the New York Fire Department in the wake of the 9-11 terrorist attacks. More than 130 bids were placed on the ticket, including one from Dallas Mavericks owner Mark Cuban. The anonymous buyer ended up giving his ticket to a 12-year-old girl from Brooklyn whose father was one of the firefighters killed in the collapse of the World Trade Center.

Deepest penetration into the stands to attack a heckler

12 rows: Vernon Maxwell, Houston, February 6, 1995
With his Rockets on the way to a 120–82 loss, Mad Max lost his cool and plunged 12 rows deep to punch a fan who had been heckling him. Maxwell accused the fan of baiting him with racial epithets about the death of his infant daughter. The fan insisted he had merely taunted Maxwell about his poor play. The Rockets player received a 10-game suspension and a $20,000 fine.

Most hostile fan reaction to the MVP of an All-Star game

Philadelphia, Kobe Bryant, Feburary 10, 2001
Considering that Kobe Bryant was raised in Philadelphia, and that his father had played for the 76ers, you might think he would have received a warm welcome at the 2001 All-Star game. Think again. The boos began in the pre-game intro-ductions and grew louder with every basket. Bryant didn't even need to score to get jeered—all he had to do was dribble the ball, and some fans cheered each of his misses. The reac-tion didn't hurt Bryant's game: the Lakers guard scored a game-high 31 points to lead the West to a 135–120 win over

the East. The booing reached a crescendo when Bryant received the MVP award after the game.

First NBA team mascot
"Go the Gorilla," Phoenix Suns, 1980
In the late 1970s a fan hired a singing-telegram gorilla to show up at a Phoenix Suns game. The gorilla sang "Happy Birthday" to the man's wife during the first-quarter break. The crowd cheered the gorilla on and it soon became a custom for locals to hire singing gorillas to come to the game. The Suns capitalized on the stunt and decided to create their own gorilla mascot. "Go" burst on the scene in 1980 and set the gold standard for mascot acrobatics.

First fan arrested for attacking a mascot
Jeff Hawkins, February 21, 2004
In the waning seconds of a game between Orlando and Denver, William Jeffrey Hawkins attacked the Magic's mascot "Stuff the Magic Dragon." Hawkins clotheslined Stuff, yanked him into the seats, and put him in a chokehold. As Orlando Police Lieutenant John O'Grady quipped, "Stuff was nearly snuffed." Hawkins, a Magic season ticket holder, later said he was so drunk that he remembered nothing of what transpired. If that's true, he forgot quite a bit, most notably the police having to use three stun gun shots to subdue him and then his own arrest for misdemeanor battery, disorderly intoxication, and resisting an officer without violence. After posting $500 bail, Hawkins stated, "I was really just trying to fun with him. I am really sorry, Stuff. Nobody would want to hurt you, my friend."

Largest mascot fine for a skit

$15,000: "Bear," Utah Jazz, February 2004

Utah was fined $15,000 by the NBA in 2004 for what was deemed to be an "inappropriate" skit that ridiculed former Jazz forward and current Los Angeles Laker Karl Malone. During a time-out, Jazz mascot "Bear" answered a fake call that was broadcast over the loudspeakers. The caller imitated Malone's voice and identified himself as "Mail," saying he wanted to come "home," that Los Angeles fans were "mean" to him, and the Lakers didn't pass him the ball. The call ended with the impersonator saying, "I guess it could be worse. I could be Ko...," stopping short of saying Kobe. Bryant had spent the previous day in court in Colorado, where he was facing a sexual assault charge. Bad taste? Perhaps. But what really wasn't funny was that the Jazz forced the man who plays the Bear to pay half the fine—$7,500— out of his own pocket. Although the skit was the mascot's idea, the team's front office, including owner Larry Miller, gave it the green light.

First mascot arrrested for selling marijuana

"Da Bull," Chicago Bulls, January 20, 2004

Chester Brewer, 31, who had worked as Chicago's furry slam-dunking mascot "Da Bull" since 1996, was busted for selling marijuana from his car in 2004. Police officers found six ounces of weed in individual plastic bags inside a paper bag in Brewer's possession, and a scale in his trunk. He was not dressed as a bull at the time of his arrest.

Age of oldest Hall of Famer to assault a mascot

69: Dolph Schayes, May 4, 1997

He may have been long retired, but 69-year-old Dolph
Schayes proved he could still connect with a hook shot. The
former NBA star was attending a 1997 playoff game to watch
his son, Danny Schayes of the Magic, when the Heat's mascot, Burnie, sprayed the Hall of Famer and other Magic fans
with a fancy squirt gun. Schayes got up from his seat and
clocked Burnie with a right hook.

Largest lawsuit filed against a mascot by a fan

$1 million: "Burnie," Miami Heat, 1994

Burnie got burned. The Heat were playing the Atlanta
Hawks in an exhibition game in San Juan, Puerto Rico, on
October 23, 1994, when Wes Lockard, dressed in his fuzzy
orange bird costume pulled a female fan out of her front row
seat during a time-out to participate in a stunt. She resisted,
fell, was helped up by the mascot, and pulled onto the court,
at which point she walked back to her seat. The woman,
Yvonne Gil de Rebollo, the wife of a local Supreme Court
justice, was not amused. She filed a lawsuit, claiming she had
suffered bruises and lingering pain in her arm and back and
emotional distress due to humiliation. "I pull people out of
the stands all the time at our place to dance," said Lockard.
"This time, I picked the wrong person." No kidding. A federal jury found in her favor and awarded $10,000 damages
against Lockard and the Heat. Unhappy with the award, Gil
de Rebollo, who had asked for $1 million in damages, peti-
tioned for and got a second trial. During the proceedings,
the Heat offered $100,000 to settle, an offer she rejected.

Eventually, the jury awarded Gil de Rebollo $50,000. Still unsatisfied, she filed for a third trial, but this time the court denied her request.

Largest chest on an unofficial mascot
88 inches: Busty Heart, Boston Celtics
Stripper Busty Heart and her massive 88-inch bazooms bounced into the public eye during Game 1 of the Celtics' 1986 playoff series with the Atlanta Hawks. The tall blonde caused a major commotion at Boston Garden when she began dancing in a tight halter top right next to a CBS TV camera. The uproar prompted Celtics radio announcer Johnny Most to explain to his listeners: "There is a blonde with very large assets dancing in the stands. She looks like Morganna but much larger." The voluptuous Heart became Boston's unofficial mascot, and from her seat near the Hawks' bench she created such a visual distraction that Atlanta coach Mike Fratello later claimed she cost his team at least one win in the series, which the Celtics took in five games.

[7]

HANG TIME

In 2004 coach Larry Brown ended the longest unfulfilled pursuit of an NBA title. After 22 years of diagramming plays without copping a ring, the 62-year-old Brown won it all with a gritty underdog, guiding his Detroit Pistons to victory over the glitzy Los Angeles Lakers in the finals.

Longest NBA game

78 minutes: Rochester vs. Indianapolis, January 6, 1951

This marathon lasted six overtimes, but it was no barn-burner. Disgusted by the stalling tactics employed by both teams, some fans booed and hundreds of others walked out of Rochester's Edgerton Park Arena. In the six overtimes, only 23 shots were taken. At the start of each overtime, the team that earned the tip simply played keep-away—one player dribbled or held the ball and looked around hoping to make the smart pass for a high percentage shot. Indianapolis won the snoozefest 75–73.

Latest starting time for an NBA game

Midnight: Boston vs. Fort Wayne, February 21, 1952

As a marketing ploy this left something to be desired. The Celtics and Pistons tipped off at midnight in a "Milkman's Special" following an Ice Follies show at Boston Garden. (In that era milkmen rose early to deliver milk to customers' homes.) The game, which Boston won 88–67, attracted 2,368 fans, some 2,000 less than the Celtics' average gate that season.

First NBA game played outside North American time zones

Phoenix vs. Utah, November 2, 1990

The NBA became the first American professional sports league to stage regular-season games outside North America when the Phoenix Suns and Utah Jazz played two contests in Japan at the Tokyo Metropolitan Gymnasium to open the 1990–91 season. To prepare his team for the change in time zones, Suns coach Cotton Fitzsimmons began holding practices at 3 a.m. in Phoenix before his team's departure. The strategy paid off as a capacity crowd of 10,111 watched the Suns race past the Jazz 119–96 behind 38 points and 10 rebounds from Tom Chambers. The jet-lagged Jazz rebounded to win the next night's tilt 102–101.

Longest game delay caused by a seeing-eye dog
3 minutes: Orlando vs. Detroit, January 18, 2005
Who didn't let the dog out? The start of the second half of a Pistons-Magic game in January 2005 was delayed for three minutes after a seeing-eye dog relieved itself on the court. The dog was with Canine Companions for Independence, a charity organization that was receiving a $10,000 donation from the Orlando Magic Youth Foundation. When the Pistons came out for the second-half warm-ups, Rasheed Wallace walked up to the lane where the feces had fallen, stopped, and stared in disbelief. An arena worker was enlisted to scoop up the mess. In response to the stink, Seeing Eye Dog Inc. of New Jersey complained to the press that the canine was not a Seeing Eye dog, a brand name reserved for guide dogs trained by its company only.

Longest game delay caused by a bat
5 minutes: Houston vs. Golden State, March 8, 2002
When your point guard gets strafed by a bat, it's probably not a good omen. Play was stopped for five minutes during the second quarter of a March 2002 game between the Rockets and the Warriors when a bat emerged from the rafters at Houston's Compaq Center and buzzed Moochie Norris. The Rockets guard cringed and froze with an astounded look before referee Courtney Kirkland halted the action. The bat continued flying about, swooping and climbing, sometimes

lapping the court above the second deck before making another dive. The players, many laughing, scattered as the crowd egged on the bat. After a five-minute delay the game resumed, but the bat descended again during a time-out promotion in which children were shooting baskets. This time a ball boy snagged the intruder with a net and released it outside the arena. The Warriors battered the Rockets 108–95.

Longest game delay caused by noxious fumes

9 minutes: Boston vs. Los Angeles Clippers, March 7, 2003
The third quarter had just ended when Boston's players suddenly bolted from their bench, gagging and coughing and covering their faces with towels. The possibility of a terrorist act immediately came to mind, and in the ensuing confusion Celtics coach Jim O'Brien tried to convince the referee to postpone or cancel the rest of the game. But NBA officials, working with Boston police and FleetCenter security, decided that the substance was most likely Mace or pepper spray released as a prank. The suspected culprits were four men who abruptly left the building before fans and players began having trouble breathing. The game was resumed after a nine-minute delay. Boston won 83–72.

Longest game delay caused by fireworks

50 minutes: San Antonio vs. Golden State, November 4, 1994
The San Antonio Spurs' 1994–95 season opener was delayed by 50 minutes when a fireworks display during the player introductions triggered the Alamodome sprinkler system, including a large, high-pressure water cannon. Fans, players, and coaches were drenched by an indoor shower that lasted four minutes and distributed 12,000 gallons of

water. The Spurs got hosed in the game too, losing to
Golden State 123–118.

Longest tape delay used at a halftime show

7 seconds: NBA All-Star game, February 15, 2004

Two weeks after Janet Jackson's breast-baring surprise at the
Super Bowl, Beyonce was scheduled to shake it at halftime
of the 2004 NBA All-Star game. To prevent another flash
of flesh, TNT used a seven-second tape delay. If anything,
Beyonce's performance was more risque than Jackson's.
After descending from the ceiling while singing the Donna
Summer disco hit "Love to Love You Baby," she made her
way to a platform in the middle of the court and gyrated
suggestively in a deep V-neck halter dress in front of a wind
machine. Beyonce's lively dancing nearly exposed her breasts,
but not quite. At least, not as far as we know.

Longest time needed to play the final three seconds of a game

*4 months: San Antonio vs. Los Angeles,
November 30, 1982 to April 13, 1983*

Play it again, Sam. On November 30, 1982, the Spurs lost a
137–132 double-overtime game to the Lakers, but protested
that the outcome was tainted by a play that occurred with
three seconds left in regulation. The Spurs led 116–114,
with Laker Norm Nixon at the line for the second of two free
throws. Instead of releasing the ball, Nixon faked a shot,
drawing members of both teams into the lane. After some
debate, a double-lane violation was called by the officials and
a jump ball was held at center court. Los Angeles controlled
the tip and scored the game-tying basket. The Spurs argued
that the correct call should have been to make Nixon shoot

the free throw. The league agreed and the final three seconds of the game were replayed—four months later when the teams next met in San Antonio. The Spurs won—not only that game 117–114—but also the scheduled one, which was played after the protested contest, 114–109.

First NBA game postponed by rain
Seattle vs. Phoenix, January 5, 1986
Although common in baseball, a basketball postponement due to rain is a rarity. To date, it's only happened once in the NBA. A heavy downpour and the Seattle Center Coliseum's leaky roof were to blame for the stoppage, as the Suns and Sonics were finally sent home in the second quarter. The game was completed the next day, with Phoenix winning 117–114.

Strangest minute of silence request by a coach
Phil Jackson, Chicago, June 1996
Jackson was famed for his application of meditation and other spiritual practices to the art of coaching. During the 1996 NBA playoffs, he huddled the Bulls players together at practice one day to observe a minute of silence in honor of one of his recently deceased heroes: wigged-out LSD pioneer Timothy Leary.

Most mathematically complex explanation for a rule change
The 24-second shot clock: 1954
Danny Biasone, owner of the NBA's Syracuse Nationals, invented the shot clock after the 1953–54 season in an attempt to speed up the game and prevent teams from stalling. The lack of pace in NBA games in the early 1950s

was widespread, as the standard strategy was to get a lead and then play keep-away. Biasone chose 24 seconds as his cut-off point by a mathematical formula. Figuring that the average number of shots two teams would take during a game was 120, he then divided that number into 48 minutes or 2,880 seconds, the length of a game, and came up with the magical figure of 24. This bit of inspired reckoning produced a revolution. During the first season of the 24-second clock, teams averaged 93.1 points per game, a jump of 13.6 points from the previous year. In 1954–55, the Boston Celtics became the first NBA team to average more than 100 points for an entire season, and four years later every team topped that plateau.

First player beaned by a shot clock
Shaquille O'Neal, Orlando, April 23, 1993
O'Neal rammed home a dunk so powerful that it shredded a backboard's support braces, causing a Nets-Magic game at Meadowlands Arena to be delayed more than 45 minutes. The backboard, stanchion, and base all had to be replaced. "I just went up and dunked and it broke," O'Neal explained. "It really came crashing down. The shot clock hit me in the head. It hurt a little bit, but not that much. I have a hard head."

Longest NBA career (including playoffs)
66,297 minutes: Kareem Abdul-Jabbar, 1969–70 to 1988–89
Although Robert Parish holds the NBA mark for most career games with 1,611, if you include playoff contests, then Abdul-Jabbar tops Parish by two, 1,797 to 1,795. The lanky seven-foot-two center was one of the first pros to take a scientific approach to physical conditioning, and that factor

helped him play more minutes than anyone in history. At age 38, Abdul-Jabbar led the Lakers to the 1985 title, becoming the oldest player to win a playoff MVP award.

Shortest NBA career

1 minute: Forest Able, Syracuse, 1956–57
1 minute: Dave Scholz, Philadelphia, 1969–70
1 minute: Barry Sumpter, Los Angeles Clippers, 1988–89
1 minute: Cedric Hunter, Charlotte, 1991–92
1 minute: Andy Panko, Atlanta, 2000–01

To say these guys had brief careers doesn't quite capture it. They didn't even have time to work up a sweat. Of the five, only Scholz scored a basket, giving him a career average of two points per minute. Able had the busiest minute. In his moment in the sun with Syracuse, he attempted two shots and collected one rebound, one assist, and one personal foul.

Longest retirement before returning to play

7 years: Bob Cousy, 1963 to 1970

In 1969, six years after he retired as the NBA's all-time assists leader, Cousy was appointed coach of the Cincinnati Royals. By coincidence, the team was led by guard Oscar Roberston, who had just eclipsed Cousy's NBA record for career assists. In his second year as Royals coach, the 42-year-old Cousy suited up and played seven games in a bid to generate fan interest. With Cousy and Robertson manning the backcourt, the Royals boasted the two highest-scoring set-up men in NBA history.

Fastest foul-out, one game

3 minutes: Bubba Wells, Dallas, December 29, 1997
It was the "Hack a Worm" strategy. Mired in an 11-game
losing streak and faced with the onerous chore of playing the
first-place Chicago Bulls, Dallas Mavericks coach Don Nelson dispatched seldom-used rookie Charles "Bubba" Wells
late in the game with the sole purpose of fouling Dennis
Rodman until he ran out of lives. Nelson figured that Rodman, a notoriously poor free-throw shooter, was sure to
misfire just enough at the charity stripe to gift wrap a victory
for the Mavs. Wells followed his instructions to the letter,
fouling out after just three minutes, laying waste to the previous record of five minutes set by Syracuse's Dick Farley in
1956. Meanwhile, Rodman made nine of 12 free throws and
the Bulls took the game 111–105.

Latest three-pointer scored in an NBA game

0.1 second: Trent Tucker, New York, January 15, 1990
There was a mere one-tenth of a second left in a 106–106
game between Chicago and New York in 1990 when Trent
Tucker gathered an inbounds pass, turned, fired, and hit a
three-pointer to sink the Bulls. The Bulls couldn't believe
that Tucker could accomplish all of that in one-tenth of a
second. Neither did the NBA. The next season, the league
passed a rule that stated: "Three-tenths of a second is needed
on the clock to catch the ball and shoot it into the basket
whether the shot is made or not."

Latest buzzer-beater in a championship game

*0.7 seconds: Vinny "the Microwave" Johnson,
Detroit, June 14, 1990*

Johnson earned his nickname during the 1980s with the Pistons because he was able to come off the bench and heat up quickly. Johnson's biggest bucket came in Game 5 of the 1990 finals against Portland when the "Microwave" sparked a late Motown surge, then capped the rally by sinking a 14-footer with 0.7 seconds left to seal a 92–90 triumph and give Detroit a second straight championship.

Most points scored by a player in the last 35 seconds of a game

13: Tracy McGrady, Houston, December 9, 2004

McGrady's nickname is the "Big Sleep," but there was nothing sleepy about his 35-second, 13-point burst of lightning on December 9, 2004. McGrady drained four difficult three-pointers, the last one a running jumper with 1.7 seconds left to propel the Rockets to an 81–80 shocker over San Antonio. "The rim felt really big to me out there," said McGrady, who had a game-high 33 points.

Most electifying scoring suge by a player in the last nine seconds of a playoff game

Reggie Miller, Indiana, May 7, 1995

Miller needed only 8.9 seconds to establish his legend as a Knicks killer. The Pacers looked to be dead, down by six points with 16 seconds to play, when Miller hit a three. Seconds later, the skinny guard stole an inbounds pass. Instead of settling for an open two, Miller deliberately dribbled back to the three-point line and launched a three. His hoop-splitter knotted the game. But there was more to come.

A few moments later, Miller was fouled pulling down a defensive rebound. He nailed his two free throws, and the Knicks didn't score again. After the 107–105 win, Miller allegedly shouted "Choke artists! Choke artists!" at Knicks fans as he ran through the exit tunnel.

Highest minutes-per-game average, one season
48.5: Wilt Chamberlain, Philadelphia, 1961–62
Conventional wisdom suggests that players have to rest during games or else they will wear down during a season. Conventional wisdom didn't apply to Chamberlain. The center averaged 48.5 minutes per game in 1961–62, a pretty amazing feat considering that a standard game is 48 minutes long. He also posted a paranormal average of 50.4 points per game. The Warriors played a total of 10 overtime periods in seven games and Chamberlain was on the court for 3,882 of a possible 3,890 minutes. Of the team's 80 games, he went the distance in 79 of them.

Most minutes played, one game
69: Dale Ellis, Seattle, November 9, 1989
Ellis did all he could, scoring a career-high 53 points and logging a record 69 minutes of court time, but it still wasn't enough to produce a win. Milwaukee outlasted Seattle 155–154 in the NBA's only five-overtime game since the advent of the 24-second shot clock in 1954.

Most combined minutes played for opposing teams, one game
15: Ralph Sampson, Philadelphia and
New Jersey, March 23, 1979
It was the last word in tape delay. The Philadelphia 76ers

and the New Jersey Nets began a game on November 8, 1978—but had to wait four months for the final result. The Nets filed a protest after coach Kevin Loughery and star forward Bernard King were assessed three technical fouls each in the third quarter. The league upheld the appeal and ordered the final 17:50 of the game to be replayed on March 23, 1979. But before it was replayed, the Nets and Sixers completed a trade that sent Ralph Sampson to New Jersey and Eric Money and Harvey Catchings to Philadelphia. All three suited up for their new teams in the carryover game, but Sampson logged the most minutes. It marked the only time in the history of professional sports that a player officially played for both teams in the same game.

Longest wait by a player before winning a championship

19 years: Kevin Willis, 1984 to 2003

When the San Antonio Spurs captured the 2003 NBA title it was 40-year-old center Kevin Willis who carried the championship trophy into the locker room. Asked how it felt, Willis replied: "It was light. Everything feels light. All the love I have for the game, and all the work it took to get here, it was worth it." His wait, the longest in NBA history, lasted 19 years.

Shortest wait by a city between NBA franchises

1 year: Philadelphia, 1962 to 1963

The Philadelphia Warriors moved to San Francisco in 1962, but the basketball void in the City of Brotherly Love did not last long. One year later, the Syracuse Nationals franchise, which had been one of the Warriors' most bitter rivals, was purchased by paper manufacturer Irv Kosloff and attorney

Ike Richman, who moved the team to Philadelphia and renamed it the 76ers.

Longest wait by a city between NBA franchises

48 years, Toronto, 1947 to 1995

The Toronto Huskies were a charter member of the Basketball Association of America, which later evolved into the NBA. In fact, the league's first game was played in Toronto on November 1, 1946, when the Huskies were beaten 68–66 by the New York Knicks at Toronto's Maple Leaf Gardens. The Huskies folded after only one season, and it was not until November 3, 1995, that a Toronto team hosted its next NBA tilt when the Raptors topped New Jersey 94–78 at the SkyDome.

Longest wait by a team before winning its first NBA title

41 years: Detroit Pistons, 1948–49 to 1988–89

Originally based in Fort Wayne, the Pistons joined the NBA in 1948. The team quickly became a force and when the Pistons lost the finals by a single point in Game 7 to Syracuse in 1955, it seemed only a matter of time before they would claim the crown. But things didn't go as expected. After moving to Detroit in 1957, the club slipped into the haze of mediocrity and it didn't emerge from the mist until 30 years later. Finally, in 1989, the Chuck Daly–coached Pistons nailed down that first elusive title.

Shortest wait by a team before winning its first NBA title

3 years: Milwaukee Bucks, 1968–69 to 1970–71

The Bucks bounded to the top in their third season thanks largely to the presence of two players: 23-year-old center

Lew Alcindor and newly acquired 33-year-old guard Oscar Roberston. In just his second season, Alcindor led the league in scoring and was voted league MVP, while Robertson furnished consummate ballhandling, outside shooting, and backcourt leadership. The Bucks led the league with a 66–16 mark and rolled to the title, losing only two games in the postseason.

Longest wait by a team to make its first playoff appearance

9 years: Utah Jazz, 1974–75 to 1982–83
8 years: Memphis Grizzlies, 1995–96 to 2002–03
Neither of these two franchises survived their droughts in their original sites. The Jazz, which began life in New Orleans in 1974, fled to Mormon country in 1979. The Grizzlies suffered through six miserable seasons in Vancouver before escaping to Elvis country in 2001.

Longest wait by a team between playoff games, one postseason

12 days: Los Angeles Lakers, 1982
Because Los Angeles swept its first two playoff opponents in 1982 and because the Eastern Conference champion Philadelphia 76ers struggled to defeat theirs, Pat Riley's boys had to wait a record 12 days before beginning the finals. Long layoffs are supposed to be the kiss of death for teams in the postseason, but Riley kept his team active with twice-daily practices, and the Lakers won the title in six games.

[8]

JUST
VISITING
FROM HELL

Since joining the NBA in 1990, Derrick Coleman has been arrested for
drunk driving, trespassing, battering a
woman, beating up a 17-year-old for
saying, "The Nets stink," and for uri-
nating in front of diners at a restau-
rant. "It's unfortunate that I can't
function as a normal person in today's
society," said Coleman. Hard to argue
with that.

Most criminal charges accumulated in one day by an MVP

14: Allen Iverson, Philadelphia, July 2002

Iverson racked up 14 criminal charges after he and his uncle, Gregory, both armed with guns, allegedly barged into the West Philadelphia apartment of his cousin, Shaun Bowman, in the middle of the night on July 3, 2002. The NBA's 2001 MVP was hunting for his wife, Tawanna, who had been in hiding for two days after he tossed her out on the street, naked, during an argument. Iverson was charged with aggravated and simple assault, reckless endangering of other people, conspiracy, possession of an instrument of crime, weapons violations, burglary, and criminal trespass. The case was serious; if convicted on all counts, he faced more than 50 years in prison. But Iverson didn't serve a single day. Charges were dropped because the key witnesses refused to testify against him. The notoriety was good for Iverson's bank balance, as sales of his Reebok athletic gear soared.

Most weapons mentioned in a pre-game diatribe

6: Kevin Garnett: Minnesota, May 19, 2004

Maybe Garnett missed his calling. Rather than a basketball player, he sounded like a soldier of fortune when he riffed to a reporter on his mind-set prior to Minnesota's Game 7 playoff game against Sacramento in 2004. "It's Game 7, man. That's it. It's for all the marbles. Sitting in the house, I'm loadin' up the pump [shotgun]. I'm loadin' up the Uzi. I got a couple M-16s, a couple 9s [handguns]. I got a couple joints with some silencers on them. I'm just loading clips, a couple grenades. I got a missile launcher with a couple of missiles. I'm ready for war." Combat metaphors aside, Garnett did come through in the clutch, scoring 32 points and snaring

21 rebounds to carry his club to an 83–80 victory
and a berth in the Western Conference finals.

Longest stream of profanities directed at an owner, one game
Latrell Sprewell, Minnesota, December 23, 2003
It was Sprewell's Christmas gift to New York. The former
Knick was making his first visit to Madison Square Garden
since the club traded him to Minnesota. James Dolan, the
Knicks' chairman and CEO of the Garden, had questioned
Sprewell's character when the trade was made and Sprewell
didn't forget. He began barking expletives at Dolan, who
was sitting near the Knicks' bench with his wife, Kristin, in
the first quarter, and didn't let up throughout the Wolves'
98–92 victory. Afterward, an irate Dolan said, "All I can tell
you is that he doesn't belong in our stadium." Not all of the
Knicks were upset by the squalid display. "Every guy tends
to lose it from time to time" said Kurt Thomas. "You can't
hold it against him." The NBA decided otherwise. It fined
Sprewell $25,000. Sprewell had no regrets. "I'm so used to
fines," he said. "They think that bothers me?"

Weakest team response to a player's tantrum
Portland Trail Blazers, January 2005
Want to coach in Portland? After Blazers coach Maurice
Cheeks criticized Darius Miles for his lackluster defensive
play at a team meeting on January 27, 2005, the player went
ballistic, unleashing a salvo of racial invectives and threats
in Cheek's direction. The *Oregonian* newspaper reported
that Miles used the N-word "at least 20 times" during the
confrontation. In a tepid response, Portland suspended
Miles for a mere two games. A few weeks later, a confidential

document was leaked to the media that indicated that the Blazers had agreed to repay Miles the $150,000, plus interest, that he lost due to his suspension in return for him not filing an official grievance. Shortly after this news hit the club took more decisive action—it fired Cheeks.

Most convictions for impersonating a police officer, one season
2: Olden Polynice, Utah, 2000

Polynice holds the unique distinction of being busted for impersonating a police officer twice within a span of two months in 2000. In the first case, Mark and Patti Schneller said they were driving in downtown Salt Lake City when a car sped past them and almost hit them. Mark Schneller responded by making a rude gesture, prompting the other car to stop. The driver, identified by the Schnellers as Polynice, flashed a badge and said: "I'm with the California Sheriff's Office and I can have you arrested." (The badge Polynice used was an honorary shield given to him by the Los Angeles Police Department.) In the second instance, Polynice pursued a couple (that he said had cut him off) all the way to their home, where he verbally abused them, claiming to be a police officer and again flashing his badge. The couple didn't recognize the six-foot-ten black man as a Jazz player, but wrote down his license plate, allowing investigators to track him down. Utah team president Dennis Haslam initially defended Polynice, stating: "I don't see this as a big deal. Frankly, I look at Olden as probably a victim. That we are to think he tried to impersonate himself as a police officer is pretty silly." It may have been silly, but Polynice eventually admitted his guilt. He got off easy, receiving 18 months' probation, a $500 fine, and an order to perform community service. The news reports did not say if he had to turn in his badge.

Most games missed by feigning an injury to avoid arrest

2: Vernon Maxwell, San Antonio, 1997

Maxwell's two-game stint on the injured list during the
1996–97 season was completely bogus, but it was warranted
nonetheless. He feigned injuries to get out of playing games
in Orlando and Miami because warrants had been issued for
him in the state of Florida for failure to pay child support.
Maxwell eventually settled the case after forking out
$51,000 in back pay.

Most chauffeurs killed by a former NBA player

1: Jayson Williams, February 2002

At 2:00 a.m. on February 14, 2002, the former NBA star
brought several visitors, including four members of the
Harlem Globetrotters, to his home, a sprawling 41-room
mansion northwest of Trenton, New Jersey. Thirty minutes
later, a shotgun blast shook the house. Several visitors rushed
into Williams's bedroom and found his chauffeur, Gus
Christofi, slumped against a wall, dying from a massive chest
wound. A shotgun lay on the floor nearby. At 2:38 a.m.,
Williams's adopted brother, Santiago, called 911 and
reported the death as a suicide. About the same time, some
guests saw Williams and another man trying to place
Christofi's palm print and fingerprints on the shotgun. Later,
according to the witnesses, Williams changed clothes and
disposed of the bloody ones he was wearing when the driver
was shot. Williams was charged with aggravated manslaughter and other gun-related felonies, and the case went to trial
in 2004. Williams's lawyer argued that Christofi's death was
purely accidental. He said that Williams was unaware that
the chauffeur was in the path of the shotgun when he flipped

it shut, causing the weapon to fire. The jury cleared Williams of the most serious charge of aggravated manslaughter, deadlocked on a charge of reckless manslaughter, but did convict him of trying to cover up Christofi's death as a suicide.

Only player to admit to plotting to murder his coach
Spencer Haywood, Los Angeles, 1980

Haywood's spectacular talents were often overshadowed by the controversy he generated. He won his lone NBA championship with the Lakers in 1979–80, but it was not exactly a fond experience. At the time, he was known as Hollywood Haywood, was married to model Iman, and was addicted to crack cocaine. Lakers coach Paul Westhead finally threw Haywood off the squad during the finals after he passed out during a practice. In a drug-induced haze, the forward began plotting revenge. In his autobiography *Spencer Haywood: The Rise, The Fall, The Recovery,* he claimed that he planned to murder Westhead by cutting the brake cables on his car. Haywood's mother talked him out of the plot.

Most money lost by strangling a coach
$6.4 million: Latrell Sprewell, Golden State, 1997–98

Sprewell and his coach P.J. Carlesimo had been feuding for weeks before things came to a head during a practice on December 1, 1997, when Sprewell objected to Carlesimo's admonition "to put a little mustard on those passes." As the coach approached Sprewell, the six-foot-five guard warned, "Don't come up on me! Don't come up on me!" When Carlesimo continued walking forward, Sprewell grabbed him by the throat, dragging him to the ground and choking him for several seconds before other players tore his hands away.

Twenty minutes later, Sprewell returned and went after Carlesimo again, connecting with a glancing blow before he could be hauled away. Golden State promptly terminated Sprewell's four-year, $32-million contract, which had nearly three years and $25 million remaining on it. Management claimed he had violated a section in the standard players' contract which states that players "must conform to standards of good citizenship and good moral character" and prohibits "engaging in acts of moral turpitude." NBA commissioner David Stern suspended Sprewell for 12 months, the longest non-drug-related penalty in NBA history. When Sprewell's lawyers and the NBA Players Association protested the severity of the punishment, the case was handed to arbitrator John Feerick. He ruled that Stern's penalty was excessive, reduced Sprewell's suspension to seven months, and reinstated his contract. Sprewell still had to forfeit $6.4 million in salary for the 1997–98 season, but the Warriors were forced to pay him $17.3 million for the last two years of his contract—unless they traded him, which is exactly what they did, sending their coach strangler to the New York Knicks.

Most money lost by head-butting a referee
$228,000: Dennis Rodman, Chicago, March 17, 1996
Maybe he forgot to take his medication. After being ejected during the first quarter against New Jersey, Rodman vented his frustration by head-butting referee Ted Bernhardt, knocking over a watercooler, stripping off his jersey, and unleashing an obscenity-laced tirade before finally leaving the court. "They can suspend me and make an example out of Dennis Rodman, I don't care," the Bulls forward said after

the game. "If I butted him, I butted him. So suspend me, David Stern. Suspend me, Rod Thorn. You guys are so big, suspend me." The NBA did just that, slapping Rodman with a $20,000 fine and a six-game suspension. Six games seemed rather mild, considering that Rodman, a repeat offender, physically assaulted a referee and that NBA vice-president Thorn was at the game and witnessed the tantrum. Along with his $20,000 fine and an automatic $1,000 fine for his ejection, Rodman lost $34,500 in salary for each game he was suspended. In total, the incident cost him $228,000.

Most expensive camera destroyed by a player during a game
$100,000: Ron Artest, Indiana, January 3, 2003
There are fiery competitors and then there are volcanoes like Ron Artest. After a 98–96 loss to the Knicks in 2003, the short-fused Pacer stormed off the court, grabbed a TV monitor, and tossed it. He then zeroed in on a cameraman who had been filming his tantrum, yanked the $100,000 camera out of his hands, and smashed it into pieces on the floor. The lens was worth $60,000 alone. Artest was suspended for three games without pay and fined $35,000. "Obviously, Ron is an emotional guy and hopefully he'll learn from it," said teammate Jermaine O'Neal. "I'm pretty sure the bill will help him learn from his mistake." Uh, not quite. In the next two months, Artest earned five more suspensions due to emotional outbursts for a total of $150,000 in fines, plus $250,000 in lost salary for the 12 games he missed.

Largest fine for kicking a photographer in the testicles

$25,000: Dennis Rodman, Chicago, January 17, 1997

Add this one to the list of lowlight reels. During a 1997 game, Rodman chased a loose basketball out of bounds and ran into a courtside cameraman. The photographer, Eugene Amos, who was seated on the floor beneath the basket, had done nothing to provoke the Worm's wrath, but that didn't stop Rodman from booting him in the gonads. Amos was dramatically carried out on a stretcher. The NBA kicked Rodman with a $25,000 fine. In addition, he paid Amos $200,000 to avoid a lawsuit. But Amos's suffering wasn't over. He was later audited by the IRS and ordered to pay $80,000 in undeclared taxes from the Rodman settlement.

First player arrested for throwing a bar patron through a window

Charles Barkley, Houston, October 6, 1997

Smash! Barkley was charged for aggravated battery and re-sisting arrest after throwing 20-year-old Jorge Lugo through a plate-glass window in an Orlando, Florida, nightclub in 1997. Lugo evidently sparked Barkley's ire by throwing some ice at a woman who was sitting with the Rockets for-ward. Barkley pleaded no contest to a misdemeanor charge of resisting arrest without violence in exchange for the dismissal of three more serious charges. He reportedly per-suaded Lugo to drop the assault charges by paying him $75,000. Barkley was unapologetic about his actions, stat-ing, "I only regret we weren't on a higher floor." The Orlando smash-up was the fourth violent public confrontation that Barkley had been involved in. Although the NBA didn't sus-pend him after this incident, it threatened to end his career unless he hired a bodyguard. Barkley took the advice.

First player suspended for engaging in dogfighting

Qyntel Woods, Portland, October 2004

This is getting into Caligula territory. Woods was investigated for staging dogfights at his home after he dumped a battle-scarred pit bull on a Portland street in October 2004. The two-year-old female had fresh puncture wounds, scars, and bruises on her chest, belly, and legs. In a subsequent search of Woods's home, police found six pit bulls, a treadmill, metal chains, and a room with bloody stains and dog prints. If found guilty of dogfighting, Woods faced a five-year prison term and up to $100,000 in fines. In January 2005 Woods pleaded guilty to a lesser charge of animal abuse and received 12 months' probation and 80 hours of community service. The Blazers, who had suspended Woods without pay when the allegations surfaced, waived him after his guilty plea. A few days later, he was signed by Miami.

First former player to admit to carrying a gun into the locker room

Greg Anthony, 2003

Anthony, a former NBA guard turned ESPN analyst, said he carried registered guns during the early part of his career in the early 1990s, as did some teammates. Anthony estimated that perhaps one in 25 NBA players had guns during the era. He also said that by the time he retired in 2000, the number had tripled. "Right or wrong, it's just the reality," Anthony said. "More athletes are worried about their safety. More and more people approach you, and you just never know what somebody is capable of doing. Players want that extra sense of security in this environment. They see carrying as a deterrent." Anthony said he had often taken a revolver secretly into the locker room when he played for the Knicks. "No one ever saw it, and I didn't know anyone even knew about it."

First player to challenge a team bus

Chris Mills, Golden State, December 20, 2002

A melee erupted at the end of a 2002 NBA game when
Portland's Bonzi Wells punched Golden State's Chris Mills
in the back of the head. Mills was so incensed he had to be
restrained from trying to get into the Blazers locker room.
The forward didn't cool down after showering. Instead, he
and some friends blocked Portland's team bus with his car
and demanded Wells come out to fight. Denied in his
attempt, he then followed the bus to the airport, unnerving
Blazers players, who ducked down in their seats in fear that
gunfire might occur. Mills got a three-game suspension.

First player arrested for inciting a riot

Anthony Mason, Charlotte, July 3, 2000

It's a unique charge, you must admit. According to police
accounts, officers were trying to separate two groups of men
arguing over women on New Orleans' Bourbon Street when
Mason slugged one officer and began rallying the crowd. The
cop who had been hit tried to subdue the six-foot-eight, 270-
pound Mason with pepper spray with no effect. When other
officers arrived, some in the crowd threw bottles and shouted
racial slurs at the police. Mason was charged with public
drunkenness, battery of a police officer, resisting
arrest, and inciting a riot—a quadruple-double. He faced six
months in jail and a $500 fine on each charge. Based on Ma-
son's rap sheet, you might have reason to believe the cops. In
1998 he was arrested for statutory rape, sexual abuse, and endangering the welfare of children. He pleaded guilty to endangering—prosecutors dropped the more serious
charges—and was ordered to perform 200 hours of community service. But the New Orleans charges were eventually

dismissed. Prosecutor Mavis Early said her office was uncertain it could convict because an investigation showed Mason's intent was "questionable" when he struck a police officer.

Most combined punches and gun shots fired at a woman
5: Eddie Griffin, Houston, October 25, 2003
Griffin was charged with aggravated assault with a deadly weapon and assault causing bodily injury in October 2003, after the six-foot-ten player punched his girlfriend three times in the face and then fired two gun shots at her car as she sped away from his Houston mansion. Griffin was angry because she had found him with another woman. At the time, the first-round draft pick was on Houston's supsended list for missing several practices and a team flight for a preseason game. The Rockets cut Griffin on December 20, 2003. Although he faced a possible 20-year prison sentence, he was quickly signed by New Jersey. But Griffin never played for the Nets. Instead, he entered an alcohol abuse program, then was jailed in early February 2004 for repeatedly violating the curfew terms of his bond, including an incident when he tried to run a man over with his SUV during an altercation outside a gas station. On February 14, he was released from jail to enter another alcohol abuse program. The Nets waived Griffin at the end of February. In March he pleaded guilty to misdemeanor assault in the Houston case and received 18 months' probation. On October 5, 2004, the troubled forward signed with Minnesota.

Longest prison sentence received by a future All-Star

15 years: Allen Iverson, 1993

While still in high school, the 17-year-old Iverson was convicted on a felony charge of "maiming-by-mob" for his role in a bowling alley brawl and received a 15-year prison sentence, with 10 years suspended. He spent four months behind bars before Virginia's first black governor, Douglas Wilder, granted him a pardon.

First player arrested by a Secret Service agent

Rodney White, Denver, September 5, 2004

What could White have been thinking? He and two friends were arrested by a Secret Service agent after they were spotted driving around Washington, D.C., firing revolvers into the air out the windows of an SUV. All three were booked for unlawful discharge of a firearm—a felony. They were also charged with five misdemeanors: carrying a pistol without a license, as well as possession of an unregistered firearm, unregistered ammunition, fireworks, and a prohibited weapon, which was identified as a knife. White spent 10 days in jail and wasn't allowed to go 30 miles outside of Washington until October 4. The day after a judge lifted White's travel ban, Denver re-signed him to a two-year contract. Nuggets GM Kiki Vandeweghe, who had prided himself on signing players who could be role models in the community, claimed that White's crime was an isolated case. "Rodney's been part of our family for two years now. He's been great, been a good player for us and been a great individual. We all make mistakes. This was something that was non-intentional. He acknowledges it was a mistake and will try to turn it into a positive."

Longest prison sentence for kidnapping a presidential assistant

6 years: Charles "Hawkeye" Whitney, January 26, 1996

An outstanding talent whose promising pro career was derailed by a knee injury, Hawkeye Whitney played just 70 NBA games for the Kansas City Kings from 1980 to 1982. He made a much bigger name for himself off the court in 1996 when he abducted a man in Alexandria, Virginia, forced him into a car, then drove him to two ATMs to withdraw $1,600. Making a bad situation even worse, the victim was a special assistant to U.S. president Bill Clinton. At Whitney's subsequent trial for kidnapping and robbery, former NBA coach John Lucas testified on Whitney's behalf, stating, "He's not a bad person; he's just doing bad things." We doubt that helped. Whitney was sentenced to six years.

Highest velocity clocked in a speeding arrest while driving impaired

125 mph: Derrick Coleman, Philadelphia, July 27, 2002

It was 3:30 a.m. when a white Land Rover sped past several police cars on a flat stretch of Interstate 696 in Farmington Hills, Michigan. Police chased the vehicle for three miles and clocked it at speeds of 125 mph in a 70-mph zone before pulling it over. Inside was Philadelphia 76ers forward Derrick Coleman, reeking of alcohol. He was asked to take a roadside sobriety test, which he failed. Coleman refused three times to take a Breathalyzer test, so police obtained a warrant to draw his blood and took him to a hospital, where a blood sample was taken about two hours after his arrest. Faced with this evidence, Coleman pleaded guilty and was sentenced to a 60-day jail sentence, which was suspended, three days of community service, nine months probation, and $1,500 worth of fines and court costs. This was not Coleman's first

DUI offense. In October 1999, when he was with the Charlotte Hornets, he was charged with drunk driving after an accident that sent him, a teammate, and another passenger to the hospital.

Only player to admit to snorting cocaine on the bench
Marvin "Bad News" Barnes, Boston, 1978–79
Barnes, who earned his nickname "Bad News" the old-fashioned way—by assaulting a college teammate with a tire iron—was a first-class talent who couldn't handle success. Those who saw him in his university days with the Providence Friars thought he could have been one of the all-time greats. Sadly, Barnes's pro career was one of fast-spiralling, albeit colorful, decline. Cocaine figured in the story. In one interview Barnes admitted, "When I was playing for the Celtics, I was snorting cocaine right there on the bench while the game was going on. I guess I don't need to say that my career didn't last much longer after that." Barnes concealed his actions by draping a towel over his head, but there was no concealing the erosion of his talent. He was out of the game after seven years.

Most players from one team arrested in a cocaine sting operation
3: Phoenix Suns, April 16, 1987
The boom was lowered on Phoenix in April 1987 when three Suns players and two ex-players were indicted on cocaine charges ranging from possession to trafficking. Those indicted were veteran center James Edwards, third-year guard Jay Humphries, and rookie guard Grant Gondrezick, plus former players Gar Heard and Mike Bratz. As well, guard Walter Davis, rookie William Bedford, and four

former Suns—Don Buse, Alvin Scott, Johnny High, and Curtis Perry—were implicated in the indictments as either witnessing drug transactions or knowing about them. Davis, High, and Scott agreed to testify before a grand jury in exchange for immunity. At the same time, Davis, the highest scorer in the team's history, entered drug treatment for the second time in two years. None of the players ever served any jail time.

Highest estimate of marijuana use in the NBA

60%: Charles Oakley, Toronto, February 22, 2000

Oakley told the *New York Post* that 60 percent of NBA players indulge in the illegal weed. "You got guys out there playing high every night," he claimed. The 17-year veteran also told the *Post* that marijuana use had increased dramatically during his career. When he first broke into the league in the early 1980s, Oakley noted, "there might have been one out of six" players using the drug. "Now it's six out of 12." When queried about the accuracy of his figures, Oakley said, "It's over 50 percent and once you get over 50 you've got to go to the next number, 60." Under pressure from congressional leaders and drug-policy officials, the NBA began testing for marijuana in 1999 and reportedly nets about a dozen offenders a year (about three percent of the total tested). Although this is a far lower percentage than the one supplied by Oakley, it must be noted that the players know in advance of the date they will be tested. In other words, these are guys who can't give up reefer even when they know they will be caught.

Most convincing imitation of Cheech and Chong by two teammates

Damon Stoudamire and Rasheed Wallace,
Portland, November 2002

The scene could have been lifted from *Up in Smoke*. Near midnight on November 21, 2002, Wallace and Stoudamire, and friend Edward Smith, were pulled over for speeding down Interstate 5 in a yellow Humvee while returning from a game in Seattle. When Stoudamire, who was sitting in the passenger's seat, rolled down his window, the stench of marijuana poured out. Washington State trooper Rob Huss asked Stoudamire to step out of the vehicle. The Trail Blazer's eyes were bloodshot and glazed and he reeked of marijuana and booze. Stoudamire admitted there had been some pot inside the Humvee, but he insisted it was all gone. A second trooper arrived and asked Wallace and Smith to exit the Humvee. In the process, he questioned Wallace about the marijuana smell. "We smoked it all up," said Wallace. The odor was so overwhelming that the officers could not use the K9 dog that had been brought to the scene because his senses would have been overwhelmed. A search of the car revealed marijuana beneath the front seat and in front of the passenger's seat, in the glove box, and in a seat pouch. Both players were charged with possession, and prosecuting attorney Jeremy Randolph vowed, "If they're convicted, they'll do the time." The case never made it to court. Randolph agreed to place both players on probation and drop the charges if the two committed no criminal acts for one year.

Most bags of marijuana found in a player's car

19: Sam Mack, July 2003

Mack's nine-year NBA career came to an end when the swing-man was arrested for marijuana possession. Mack attracted police attention by running a stop sign and then refusing to pull over, prompting a high-speed car chase through a Chicago suburb that reached speeds of 70 mph. After six blocks, police forced Mack to pull over his Range Rover and arrested him. Inside his car they found 19 bags of weed, a chunk of cocaine, and a scale.

Dumbest drug bust

Damon Stoudamire, Portland, July 7, 2002

They say that smoking weed makes you forgetful. Stoudamire forgot to bring his brain along with him when he attempted to pass through an airport metal detector in Tuscon with 40 grams of marijuana wrapped in aluminum foil. Naturally, the machine went off. Told to empty his pockets, Stoudamire tossed his foil-wrapped stash into the tray. "What's that?" he was asked by a security guard. "You know what it is," he replied. This marked Stoudamire's third arrest for marijuana possession in 18 months. Portland initially suspended Stoudamire and fined him $200,000 after the airport bust, but the suspension and fine were later rescinded after he entered a drug treatment program and donated $10,000 to charity.

[9]

FLYING THE
COLORS

Chicago Bulls assistant coach Tex Winter once scolded Michael Jordan for trying to do too much by himself, telling him, "There's no 'I' in the word team." The Bulls star shot back, "Maybe not, but there is in the word win." All of the vowels are included in this chapter on team records.

Longest odds overcome by a team in an NBA draft lottery

66 to 1: Orlando Magic, 1993

Orlando possessed the magic touch at the NBA draft lottery two years in a row. In 1992, the 21–61 Magic had 10 of the 66 ping-pong balls in the hopper, but ended up winning the coveted No. 1 pick and drafting Shaquille O'Neal. The hulking center helped Orlando to a 20-win improvement in 1992–93 and the club just missed the playoffs. With the best record among non-playoff teams, Orlando had the worst chance of winning first pick in the 1993 lottery. Only one of the 66 balls had Orlando's name on it. Miraculously, that ball came up and the Magic had its second straight No. 1 overall pick. The club selected Michigan forward Chris Webber, then traded him to the Warriors for the draft rights to the No. 3 pick, Memphis guard Penny Hardaway, and three future draft picks.

Most first-round draft picks lost in a bidding war, one season

2: Atlanta Hawks, 1975

In 1973–74, the Hawks finished 35–47 and missed the postseason for the first time in 12 years. In response, management decided to rebuild. Star guard Pete Maravich was traded to the New Orleans Jazz for several players and draft picks, and after winning only 31 games the next year, Atlanta owned both the No. 1 and No. 3 picks in the 1975 NBA draft. The Hawks selected David Thompson of North Carolina State and Marvin Webster of Morgan State. But both players spurned Atlanta to sign with the ABA's Denver Nuggets. Thompson became a basketball leaping legend, while Webster, who was called "the Human Eraser," developed into a top defensive specialist. The hamstrung Hawks finished the 1975–76 season at 29–53 and went 31–51 the year after that.

Only team to draft a paralyzed player
Boston Celtics, June 29, 1982

Indiana's Landon Turner was paralyzed in a car accident just prior to the 1982 draft, a few months after his team won the NCAA title. As a favor to Indiana coach Bobby Knight (who started a fund that raised $400,000 to defray Turner's medical expenses), and to lift Turner's spirits, Celtics GM Red Auerbach drafted him in the 10th round. In 1989, Turner received the Coors Light U.S. Basketball Writers Association's Most Courageous Award after returning to the court with a wheelchair basketball team. Today he is a motivational speaker in Indianapolis.

Only team forbidden to make trades without the NBA'S approval
Cleveland Cavaliers, 1983

A terrible darkness descended over Cleveland in 1980 when wealthy but wacko Ted Stepien bought the team. Acting as a hybrid owner/GM, Stepien hired and fired coaches willynilly and made a series of idiotic trades that cost the Cavs several years of first-round draft picks, nearly destroying the franchise. Stepien had a knack for disaster. After buying a softball team in 1980, he staged a promotional stunt by dropping softballs off the Terminal Tower, Cleveland's tallest building. The plunging spheres broke a woman's arm, bruised another guy's shoulder, and smashed two cars. The NBA considered Stepien such a menace that it banned him from making trades without the league's approval and eventually pressured him into selling out. In order to attract a local owner (Gordon Gund), the league had to sweeten the deal by giving the Cavaliers four bonus first-round draft picks from 1983 to 1986 to fill the vacuum that Stepien had created. After the sale was completed, the NBA passed a rule prohibiting any team from making trades that would result in that team not having a first-round pick in consecutive years. It's called the "Ted Stepien rule."

Most disastrous team sale
Buffalo Braves to John Y. Brown, 1976
The Braves entered 1976–77 on the cusp of greatness with a roster that boasted the 1974 and 1975 Rookies of the Year in Ernie DiGregorio and Bob McAdoo, plus All-Star forward Randy Smith. The team had also acquired ABA phenom Moses Malone and had just drafted Adrian Dantley, who would go on to win the 1977 Rookie of the Year. But behind the scenes treachery was afoot. During the summer of 1976, John Y. Brown, the owner of Kentucky Fried Chicken, bought a 50 percent stake in the Braves from owner Paul Snyder, then later purchased Snyder's remaining stake in the club. All told, Brown spent $6.2 million. The transaction included an unusual provision stating that if Brown sold any of the Braves players, the money would go to Snyder and the purchase price would be reduced. Brown quickly began gutting the team, trading Malone to Houston and McAdoo, the reigning NBA scoring champ, to New York for $3 million. Brown then sold a half interest in the franchise to Harry Mangurian for a reported $3 million. From a business standpoint it may have been a shrewd deal as Brown came away owning 50 percent of an NBA franchise for about $200,000. But the results were ruinous on the court. Buffalo chewed up

three coaches during the season and fell to second last in the Eastern Conference. A year later the decimated franchise moved to San Diego.

First team to make a code of conduct pledge to its fans
Portland Trail Blazers, August 2003

Once considered a model NBA franchise, the Trail Blazers began a slide into decline in the late 1990s, shortly after the appointment of president and GM Bob Whitsitt, who brought in a new cadre of high-salaried players with questionable character. A long litany of unsavory incidents followed, including sex offenses; arrests for drugs, drunken driving, and domestic violence; fights between teammates; verbal threats to referees; and obscene gestures to fans, which led the team to be dubbed "the Jail Blazers." Finally, in May 2003, Whitsitt was replaced by Steve Patterson, who traded troublemakers Rasheed Wallace and Bonzi Wells and announced the adoption of a 25-point code of conduct for all the organization's employees, coupled with a reduction in ticket prices, in a bid to woo back disgruntled local fans.

Most home arenas used by an NBA team, one season
7: Houston Rockets, 1971–72

When a group of investors bought the San Diego Rockets franchise and moved it to Houston in 1971, they saw dancing dollar signs. After all, Elvin Hayes, the Rockets star player, used to draw huge crowds at the University of Houston, including 50,000 at the Astrodome for a game against UCLA in 1968. But the football-mad city didn't warm to pro basketball. With attendance in the 4,000 range, the team couldn't even meet operating expenses. The Rockets played home games that year in Houston at the Astrodome and AstroHall, and at Hofheinz Pavilion on the University of Houston campus, at HemisFair Arena in San Antonio, as well as in El Paso and Waco, where legend has it that local churches drew more people than the Rockets. Houston even played a home date in San Diego to avoid playing one West Coast game against the Warriors, then coming home and having to return to the West Coast for another.

Most home games played by an NBA team in another country, one season

9: Buffalo Braves, 1973–74

Having fouled the waters in Buffalo with a pitiful 21–61 season the year before, the struggling Braves tried to expand their fan base in 1973–74 by playing nine home games in Canada at Toronto's Maple Leaf Gardens. Attendance increased, but it was not entirely due to an influx of Canadian fans. The Braves started winning thanks to the hot shooting of scoring champion Bob McAdoo. The Braves played six more games in Toronto the following year.

Largest team fine

$3.5 million: Minnesota Timberwolves, October 25, 2000

Minnesota gambled and lost big time. A $3.5-million fine, the maximum allowed under the collective bargaining agreement, was imposed on the Wolves by the NBA for making a secret deal with forward Joe Smith to circumvent the league salary cap. The league also voided Smith's contract and stripped Minnesota of five first-round draft choices, one of which was later restored.

**Most money offered in refunds to ticket
holders for missing the playoffs**

$500,000: Atlanta Hawks, October 2002

In a bold display of confidence, Atlanta offered $125 back to
each of its season ticket holders if the Hawks didn't qualify
for the 2002–03 playoffs. The idea—which was cooked up
by coach Lon Kruger—backfired. Atlanta finished 10th and
had to announce a refund of $500,000 to some 4,000 season
ticket holders. Kruger wasn't around to see it. He was fired
in mid-season.

Only NBA team saved by a telethon

Indiana Pacers, July 3, 1977

At least they didn't have to call Jerry Lewis. The Pacers had
a cash crunch after their first NBA season. There had been the
initial $3.2 million fee to join the NBA, plus a compensation
package that the Pacers had to pay to the ABA teams that
didn't survive the merger. Also, the Pacers wouldn't get to
share in NBA television revenues until 1980. In short, the
club needed money quickly or else the franchise would be lost
to another city. To help the Pacers' cause, local business leaders contributed $100,000, while radio station WTTV raised
more cash by organizing a telethon. The telethon began on
the evening of July 3. Sixteen hours later and just 10 minutes
before the show was set to go off the air, it was announced
that the team had reached its goal of 8,000 season tickets.

Only team to delay its home opener because of the Ice Capades

Cleveland Cavaliers, October 1970

Cleveland, Portland, and Buffalo all joined the NBA as
expansion teams in 1970–71, but only Cleveland had the

added handicap of having to play its first seven games on the road because the Cleveland Arena had been booked by the Ice Capades. The situation made it tough for the Cavs who had such a motley team that coach Bill Fitch wryly remarked to reporters prior to the season, "Just remember, the name is Fitch, not Houdini." The Cavs lost their first 15 games before finally beating Portland on the road, but they didn't register a home win until the 28th game of the season when they beat Buffalo.

First team to play five black players simultaneously
Chicago Packers, 1961–62
Although black players first entered the NBA in 1951, it was 10 more years before any team broke the unofficial quota system and put five black players on the court at the same time. The expansion Chicago Packers' historic quintet was composed of Walt Bellamy, Woody Sauldsberry, Horace Walker, Andy Johnson, and Sihugo Green.

Only NBA team to wear an NFL team's logo
Detroit Pistons, 1989
Featuring a cast of misfits and hard cases, the Pistons clawed their way to the top of the heap in 1989. The club's reputation as basketball's bad boys was so pervasive that Al Davis, the renegade owner of the Oakland Raiders football team, sent them silver-and-black shirts with the skull-and-crossbones logo of the Raiders. The Pistons wore the gear with pride and Detroit fans began showing up at games sporting the Raiders' pirate emblems.

Most future Hall of Famers on one team

8: Boston Celtics, 1962–63

The Lakers attracted media attention in 2003–04 by fielding
a team with four likely future Hall of Famers: Gary Payton,
Karl Malone, Shaquille O'Neal, and Kobe Bryant. But that's
half the total of Hall of Famers on the roster of the 1962–63
Celtics, whose lineup included Bill Russell, Bob Cousy, John
Havlicek, Sam Jones, Tom Heinsohn, Frank Ramsey, K.C.
Jones, and Clyde Lovellette. Even if you take into account
that Lovellette was enshrined largely because of his college
achievements, that's still quite an array of talent. No surprise,
the Celtics won the title that year.

Only team to have players finish 1–2–3 in scoring

Denver Nuggets, 1982–83

Until 1982–83, only one NBA team—the 1954–55
Philadelphia Warriors—had ever boasted the two top scorers
in one season. The Nuggets erased that mark by sweeping
the top three spots. Alex English led Denver's mile-high
offense with an average of 28.4 points per game; second was
Kiki Vandeweghe, at 26.7; and third was Kelly Tripucka,
at 26.5. Since then, no other team has had players claim the
top two spots.

First NBA team to play the Harlem Globetrotters

Minneapolis Lakers, February 19, 1948

This historic Lakers-Globetrotters game was no ordinary
exhibition. It was a battle between the best white team and
the best black team in the world. Led by six-foot-ten pivot
George Mikan, the Lakers were just beginning an NBA dynasty, while the barnstorming Globetrotters, who were much

more than simply a novelty act, were riding a 103-game unbeaten streak. The Lakers jumped out to a 32–23 lead at the half, but the Trotters changed tactics after intermission, playing a more physical game and keying on Mikan, and gradually closed the gap. In the last minute, with the score knotted at 59–59, the Trotters' ball-handling genius Marques Haynes got the ball, dribbled down the clock to a few seconds, then flipped a pass to Ermer Robinson, who drained a game-winning shot at the buzzer. The two teams would clash twice more the following winter, with the Globetrotters winning the first game and the Lakers the second. They met five more times in ensuing years, but by that point the NBA had become integrated, ending the Globetrotters' monopoly on black talent, and the Lakers won all five.

Only team to stage a doubleheader
Milwaukee Bucks, March 8, 1954
They were seeing double on March 8, 1954, when the Hawks hosted the Baltimore Bullets at Milwaukee Arena in the NBA's only two-team doubleheader. The twin bill produced nearly identical results as the Hawks won by scores of 64–54 and 65–54. Each game was shortened from 48 to 40 minutes.

First NBA team to play in the Soviet Union
Atlanta Hawks, July 25, 1988
The Hawks were one of the first NBA teams to scout and draft international players, and the team was instrumental in the development of the four-city American/Soviet All-Star team tour that brought American and Soviet players together on the same team for the first time. This initiative led to the

Hawks being the first NBA team invited to visit the Soviet Union in the summer of 1988. In the first game of the exhibition tour, Atlanta defeated the Soviet Georgia All-Stars 85–84.

First NBA team to include prayers in its pre-game routine
Charlotte Hornets, 1988 to 2002
The expansion Hornets added a crowd prayer to the usual pre-game hoopla at the direction of evangelist owner George Shinn in 1988. The praying ended after Shinn became embroiled in a messy sex scandal and moved the club to New Orleans in 2002.

Only NBA teams to swap owners
Boston Celtics and San Diego Clippers, 1978
Faced with declining attendance, Buffalo Braves owner John Y. Brown went looking for a new city for the Braves' franchise at the 1977 NBA owners' meeting. The Boston Celtics were owned by Irv Levin, a Beverly Hills resident who wanted to own a club that played closer to his home state. NBA attorney David Stern (who later became the league's commissioner) proposed a novel solution: the Buffalo Braves would move to San Diego, and Brown and Levin would flip franchises. In June 1978, NBA owners voted 21–1 in favor of the swap. The deal included a complicated seven-player trade, but the most important detail in the transaction was that Boston retained the draft rights to Larry Bird.

Only NBA team to trade a hockey player
New Jersey Nets, 1973
A weird case to be sure. It all began when Julius Erving

of the ABA's Virginia Squires signed a free-agent contract
with the NBA's Atlanta Hawks in the fall of 1972. The
Squires screamed foul and the case went to court, where a
three-judge panel ruled that Erving was contractually bound
to the Squires. Erving returned to Virginia and led the ABA
in scoring in 1972–73, but he still wanted out, and so, prior
to the 1973–74 season, the cash-strapped team traded him to
the ABA's New York Nets. Atlanta owner Tom Cousins was
furious with the turn of events. In an attempt to placate
him, Nets owner Roy Boe came up with a side deal. Boe also
owned the NHL's New York Islanders and Cousins also
owned the NHL's Atlanta Flames, so Boe sent Islanders de-
fenseman Pat Ribble and $400,000 in cash to the Flames. It
was scant consolation for Cousins. Erving went on to become
the dominant player of his era, while Ribble was a dud.

Highest home-winning percentage, one season
.976: Boston Celtics, 1985–86
Larry Bird and the Celtics were virtually invincible playing
on the parquet at Boston Garden in 1985–86, winning 40 of
41 regular-season games at home, then 10 more without a
loss in the playoffs. The Celtics lone home defeat came at the
hands of the Jack Ramsay–coached Portland Trail Blazers.

Highest road-winning percentage, one season
.816: Los Angeles Lakers, 1971–72
When you have Wilt Chamberlain at center and Jerry West
and Gail Goodrich in the backcourt, you're not hurting for
talent. The 1971–72 Lakers are best known for winning a
record 33 straight games, but they also set a record for the
highest road-winning percentage in history by going 31–7.

Most regular-season wins by a non-champion

68: Boston Celtics, 1972–73

By adding rising young stars Dave Cowens and Jo Jo White
to its veteran cast of John Havlicek, Paul Silas, Don Chaney,
Tom Sanders, and Don Nelson, Boston raced to the top of the
standings. The Celtics notched 68 victories, one shy of the
record set by the NBA champion Los Angeles Lakers the year
before. But the Celtics came unglued in the playoffs, losing
in seven games to the Knicks in the Eastern Conference
finals. No other NBA team has won so many games and not
emerged as a champion.

Lowest winning percentage by a championship team

.537: Washington Bullets, 1977–78

After going 44–38 on the season, Dick Motta's Bullets
seemed a long shot to advance very far in the playoffs. The
club had no player selected to the first or second All-Star
teams and its top scorer, Elvin Hayes, ranked 21st in the
league. But a disciplined team approach carried the Bullets
to six-game wins over San Antonio and Philadelphia in the
Eastern Conference playoffs and a seven-game squeaker over
Seattle in the finals.

Most consecutive years missing the playoffs

15: Los Angeles Clippers, 1976–77 to 1990–91

The Clippers' streak of suffering included one year in Buffalo, seven in San Diego, and another seven barren seasons in
Los Angeles. The club finally made the playoffs for the first
time in 1991–92, thanks to the coaching genius of Larry
Brown. Under Brown, the Clippers won 23 of their final 35
games to finish with a 45–37 mark, ending a run of 13
straight losing seasons.

Largest single-season increase in wins

36: San Antonio Spurs, 1996–97 to 1997–98

The Spurs set the gold standard for the most dramatic one-season turnaround in 1997–98. After going 20–62 in 1996–97, they rebounded to 56–26, a 36-win swing. There were two big reasons for the revival: seven-foot-one center David Robinson returned from injury and seven-foot forward Tim Duncan joined the club and won the Rookie of the Year award. With its Twin Towers alignment, San Antonio finished second in the Midwest Division and reached the Western Conference semifinals.

Largest single-season decline in wins

39: San Antonio Spurs, 1995–96 to 1996–97

An epidemic of injuries, most notably the loss of star center David Robinson to a broken foot, sent San Antonio into freefall in 1996–97. The club crashed from 59 to 20 wins, the steepest one-year decline in NBA history. But there was an upside. The Spurs hit paydirt in the 1997 draft lottery, landing the first overall pick, and selecting super prospect Tim Duncan.

Largest winning margin by a league leader

14 games: Milwaukee Bucks, 1970–71

Although often overlooked in discussions of the greatest NBA teams, no other club has finished as far ahead of the competition as the 1970–71 Milwaukee Bucks. Led by its Hall of Fame duo of center Lew Alcindor and guard Oscar Robertson, Milwaukee logged a 66–16 record, 14 games better than second-place New York, then breezed to the title, losing only two postseason games.

Highest points-per-game average, one season

126.5: Denver Nuggets, 1981–82

Under the direction of colorful coach Doug Moe, who
emphasized a relentless motion offense, which he described
as "playground ball with a little supervision," Denver went
nuclear in 1981–82, scoring 100 points or more in all 82
games and averaging a record 126.5 points per game. But
Denver also allowed 100 or more points in every game,
setting another league record. The lack of attention to
defense proved fatal in the playoffs, as the Nuggets were
crunched by Phoenix in the first round.

Most consecutive field goals missed from the start of a game

22: Sacramento Kings, February 4, 1987

Only one team was ready to play when the Lakers and Kings
tipped off at the Los Angeles Forum on February 4, 1987.
The comatose Kings didn't register a point until 9:04 had
elapsed in the first quarter, by which time they trailed 29–0.
At the end of the period the Lakers led 40–4 and the Kings
had yet to sink a shot from the field, going 0-for-18. They did
not hit a field goal until their 23rd attempt and eventually
lost 128–92. Coach Phil Johnson was fired after the game.

Fewest points, one game (since the advent of the shot clock)

49: Chicago Bulls, April 10, 1999

With Michael Jordan's retirement, Chicago crashed into a
harsh new reality in 1998–99, as the club staggered to a
13–37 record. Things hit rock bottom in April when, one
week after suffering a franchise record 115–68 pasting by
Orlando, the Bulls set an NBA record for ineptitude by scoring a mere 49 points in a 82–49 loss to Miami. During the

debacle Chicago hit a miserable 18 of 77 field goals, a performance that caused Bulls guard Ron Harper to muse, "I don't know what Michael would say about this."

Most points scored in a loss

184: Denver Nuggets, December 13, 1983

Although it doesn't sound possible, especially by today's anemic offensive standards, the Nuggets managed to put 184 on the board and still go home a loser. At the end of regulation time, their 1983 game against the Detroit Pistons was tied 145–145. After three overtime periods, Detroit prevailed 186–184.

Largest margin of victory, one game

68 points: Cleveland vs. Miami, December 17, 1991

In this 1991 mauling, the Cavaliers charged out to a 73–53 halftime lead behind guard Mark Price's 14 points, then continued to pour it on after the break, scoring 17 of the first 19 points in the third quarter. During the one-sided run, Heat coach Kevin Loughery benched all of his starters in disgust. Miami remained in hibernation for the rest of the game. The final tally was 148–80, as Cleveland outscored the visitors 42–13 in the fourth quarter and 75–27 in the second half. Despite the onslaught not a single Cavs player reached 20 points in the game.

[10]

SHOOTING
FROM THE
LIP

Penny Hardaway owns the record for the most twisted sense of love. After the NBA capped player salaries in 1999, the Orlando guard stated: "Guys aren't able to get $15 or $20 million a year anymore, so you have to play for the love of the game." Hardaway is not the only hoopster to set a milestone with his mouth.

Most famous catch phrase coined by a basketball coach

"It ain't over 'til the fat lady sings."
Dick Motta, Washington, April, 1978

The full quote is actually "The opera ain't over until the
fat lady sings." A San Antonio sportswriter named Dan Cook
used the line to buck up fans of the San Antonio Spurs, who
were trailing the Washington Bullets in the 1978 Eastern
Conference semifinals. The Spurs lost the series and Bullets
coach Dick Motta adopted the phrase as his own, reciting it
several times during the Bullets' underdog run to the championship. By the end of the 1978 playoffs "It's not over 'til
the fat lady sings" was known all over America.

Most comical observation about cocaine use in the NBA

"If 10 guys on the court sneezed, eight were losing money."
Bill Russell

The Celtics Hall of Famer concisely summed up pro
basketball's problem with nose candy in the 1970s.

Best point made in a losing argument

"They say that nobody is perfect. Then they tell you
practice makes perfect. I wish they'd make up their minds."
Wilt Chamberlain

Chamberlain was never keen on practice sessions. If any
player could get by without attending them, he was the guy.

Most befuddled sense of learning

"I don't think we learned a lesson;
I think it was a learning experience for us."
Shaquille O'Neal, Los Angeles, June 13, 2001

After a 100–86 win over Philadelphia in Game 4 of the 2001
finals, NBC reporter Jim Gray asked O'Neal if the Lakers had

learned a lesson from what happened to them the previous year in Indiana when they blew a championship-clinching game at home to the Pacers. O'Neal obviously didn't like the wording of the question.

Most unusual explanation for gaining weight

"We all get heavier as we get older because there's a lot more information in our heads."
Vlade Divac, Los Angeles Lakers

Divac was explaining to reporters why he reported to training camp 15 pounds overweight. In all probability, the Serbian center does not hold a degree in human anatomy.

Most psychedelic response to a painkiller

"Rainbows, white puffy clouds, doves of peace flying across the sky. Mozart on the piano, contrary motion scales, arpeggios up and down the keyboard, Beethoven—crashing thunder— it was all so beautiful. It was all so perfect."
Bill Walton, 2002

When Walton became a broadcaster the orbits of the planets shifted. In one of his zany 2002 playoff dispatches for NBA.com, the basketball analyst fondly recalled the effect of getting a pain-killing injection before a 1978 playoff game.

Most imaginative excuse for breaking a backboard

"I didn't mean to destroy it. It was the power, the Chocolate Thunder. I could feel it surging through my body, fighting to get out. I had no control over it."
Darryl Dawkins, Philadelphia, December 1979

The six-foot-eleven, 260-pound Dawkins was a scary dude. The fact that he believed he was possessed by a mystical chocolate spirit only made him even more menacing. This was his explanation for breaking his second backboard in three weeks, an action that earned him a league reprimand.

Largest stretching of the truth

"He's just like me—except he's seven foot six and Chinese."
Steve Francis, Houston, 2002

Maybe the six-foot-three Rockets point guard was trying to bridge the cultural divide. Most everyone else failed to see the similarities that existed between Francis and his seven-foot-six Shanghai-born teammate, Yao Ming.

Most straightforward sales pitch

"These are my new shoes. They're good shoes. They won't make you rich like me, they won't make you rebound like me, they definitely won't make you handsome like me. They'll only make you have shoes like me. That's it."
Charles Barkley, Phoenix, 1993

Barkley's image was based on the popular perception that he did not indulge in b.s. In this TV commercial for Nike, he did not fuel any fantasies.

Most peculiar criticism of greed

"I'm tired of hearing about money, money, money, money, money. I just want to play the game, drink Pepsi, wear Reebok."
Shaquille O'Neal, Los Angeles Lakers, 1996

It is reassuring to see that despite all his riches, O'Neal has been able to keep his priorities straight.

Weakest defense of inflated player salaries

"People don't understand. We might make a lot
of money, but we also spend a lot of money."
Patrick Ewing, New York, 1998

With the possible exception of retailers, Ewing did not
endear himself to anyone when he defended inflated NBA
player salaries during the 1998–99 lockout. At the time,
the Knicks center was earning $18.5 million a year.

Most obnoxious remark made during the 1998 NBA lockout

"If this keeps up much longer I may have to sell one of my cars."
Kenny Anderson, Boston, October 1998

You really have to feel for Kenny. If the NBA hadn't locked
out the players, he would have been taking down $5.8 mil-
lion. It may sound like a lot, but then he had to pay taxes
and assorted expenses, including $75,000 to insure his fleet
of eight Porsches, Mercedes, and Range Rovers, plus the
$150,000 yearly rent on his Beverly Hills crib. Then too,
there was his "hangin' around money" as he called it—
a mere $120,000 a year. After expenses, he was left with only
$2 million. How would he survive? "I have to start getting
tight," said Anderson.

Weakest grasp of mathematics

"Any time Detroit scores more than 100 points and holds
the other team below 100 points they almost always win."
Doug Collins, basketball commentator

Well, Collins was right most of the time.

Dimmest sense of history

"I can't really remember the names of the clubs that we went to."
Shaquille O'Neal, Los Angeles Lakers

O'Neal was asked whether he had visited the Parthenon during a holiday in Greece. Ancient ruin or disco, what's the difference?

Strangest response to a travel itinerary

"News ain't travelin' on no time machine."
Marvin "Bad News" Barnes, St. Louis (ABA), 1975

Barnes got the jitters after he learned that a team flight would depart Louisville, Kentucky, at 8 p.m. and arrive in St. Louis at 7:56 p.m. due to a time-zone change. The spooked ABA star showed his boarding card to the club's play-by-play man, a kid named Bob Costas, before heading to the car rental counter and renting wheels to make the trip to St. Loo.

Most suspect sense of direction

"We're going to turn this team around 360 degrees."
Jason Kidd, Dallas, 1994

The rookie guard was trying to make the point that the Mavericks were going to make a move up the standings—not too ambitious a promise considering that Dallas was 13–69 the previous year. Despite his confusion with degrees, Kidd was right; the Mavs improved by 23 wins.

Most inane complaint about playing for a team

"The guys miss things stateside, like grocery stores."
George Lynch, Vancouver, 1998

NBA players voiced numerous gripes about the hardships of playing for the Vancouver Grizzlies, such as higher taxes, border-crossing hassles, lack of endorsement opportunities, and the rain. But Lynch topped everyone with his ludicrous complaint that Canada's third-largest city had no groceries.

Most vivid description of an opponent's style

"They're really aggressive. They're like roaches on
bread—you drop some on the floor and, boom, they're on it."
Kevin Garnett, Minnesota, 2000

The entomological-minded Garnett was paying tribute to the suffocating defense of the Pat Riley–coached Miami Heat.

Funniest character sketch

"My initial response was to sue her for defamation
of character, but then I realized that I had no character."
Charles Barkley, Phoenix, 1994

The Round Mound of Rebound was responding to Tonya Harding's characterization of herself as "the Charles Barkley of figure skating."

Best insight into fan psychology

"Nobody roots for Goliath."
Wilt Chamberlain

Chamberlain made this point a few times in his career. When you are more than seven feet tall and supremely talented to boot, you lose the sympathy vote. Crowds came out to watch the Dipper play, but a lot of the ticket buyers also came to boo.

Most revealing admission of puzzlement

*"I don't have the first clue who's he's talking about
because all I worry about is Jerome."*
Jerome James, Seattle, 2003

This was James's reply when he heard that his coach,
Nate McMillan, had called him selfish.

Most dubious excuse for flashing the finger

"I black out sometimes."
Bonzi Wells, Portland, November 2003

During the third game of the 2003–04 season, Wells angrily
saluted the hometown fans with one finger. He strained his
credibility when he claimed to have no memory of the gesture. The Trail Blazers did not buy the amnesia act and fined
Wells $10,000.

Most dubious use of the term "personal problems"

*"That was just something I made up. I'm on vacation.
I'm drinking brews, playing golf and getting paid!"*
Vernon Maxwell, Houston, 1995

Personal problems can cover a lot of ground—family tragedy,
depression, domestic strife, money woes—and at one time or
another, Maxwell has probably qualified on all accounts. But
in this case he gave the term a new twist. After taking a
two-week hiatus due to "personal problems" in 1995, the
Rockets guard confessed that it was all a lie.

Lamest defense for assaulting a coach

"It's not like he was losing air or anything like that."
Latrell Sprewell, Golden State, March, 1998

Sprewell was trying to convince people that he did not need

anger counseling after he was suspended by the NBA for seven months for trying to strangle his coach, P.J. Carlesimo.

Most mean-spirited autograph refusal

"I don't sign on game days."
Patrick Ewing, New York, 1999
There might be a situation when Ewing's response would have made sense. This wasn't one of them. The Knicks star petulantly refused to sign autographs for seriously ill kids from the Starlight Children's Foundation at a charity luncheon. He was on the injured list at the time.

Most vitriolic message to Chinese fans

"I will shoot all you Chinese {bleeps}. Do you remember the Vietnam War? I'll kill y'all just like that."
Jason Williams, Sacramento, February 2001
How much did you pay for those courtside tickets? The Sacramento point guard delivered this profane volley to a fan of Chinese descent sitting behind the Kings' bench during a game at Golden State. Williams punctuated his remarks by pretending to shoot a machine gun. Mr. Sensitivity was fined $15,000.

Most confusing use of an acronym

"It's almost like we have ESPN."
Magic Johnson, Los Angeles Lakers
Johnson was remarking on how well he and his Lakers teammate, James Worthy, worked together on the court.

Most inappropriate mathematical comparison

"I'm like the Pythagorean theorem.
Not too many people know the answer to my game."
Shaquille O'Neal, Los Angeles, 1999

Players often get in over the heads when they start tossing around algebraic terms. Most school kids could tell O'Neal that the answer is c^2.

Most backhanded compliment

"I thank my teammates for letting their men blow by them."
Alonzo Mourning, Miami, 2000

Mourning didn't appear to be kidding when he said a few words about his teammates after winning the NBA's Defensive Player of the Year Award in 2000.

Most metaphysical coaching tip

"If you meet the Buddha in the lane, feed him the ball."
Phil Jackson, Chicago

It makes you wonder. If Buddha played basketball what position would he play?

Most honest assessment by a coach of his team's chances

"We got no shot to beat the Lakers."
Doug Moe, Denver, April 1987

Moe had been asked to handicap his 37–45 Nuggets' matchup with the 65–17 Los Angeles Lakers in the first round of the 1987 playoffs. The Lakers pulverized the Nuggets and went on to win the championship.

Most cutting coach's criticism of his own team

*"The only thing I can think of is maybe bringing
a doctor in to surgically put some heart into them."*
Byron Scott, New Jersey, January 29, 2001

Scott didn't pull any punches when asked by a reporter what
he could do to change the fortunes of his floundering Nets.

Best insight into a coach's attitude

*"I used to go through the whole routine—dress up, wear makeup, act
like a girl. Whenever someone would ask Phil Jackson if anything
I've done surprised him, he would always say, 'Yeah, it surprised me
that he needs a special tool to take his pressurized earrings out.'"*
Dennis Rodman, on Bulls coach Phil Jackson

Jackson was able to get the best out of the mercurial Rodman by ignoring most of his crazy antics. Only a guy with
some serious inner calm could manage it.

Best summation of the life of an expansion coach

"War is hell, but expansion is worse."
Bill Fitch, Cleveland, 1971

Fitch started his NBA coaching career the hard way—with
the expansion Cleveland Cavaliers. The clownish Cavs won
just two of their first 35 games in their inaugural season in
1971–72.

Most sadomasochistic comment

*"I loved it. It felt good. To get elbowed in
the face again, I missed that, you know."*
Elton Brand, Los Angeles Clippers, 2002

Brand evidently enjoyed picking up a split lip in his first
practice of the 2002–03 season after he missed a month with
a broken foot.

Most awkward greeting by a rookie

"Houston, I am come."
Yao Ming, 2002

Yao introduced himself to the folks in Texas via satellite
from Shanghai with these four words after he was drafted
No. 1 overall by the Houston Rockets in the 2002 NBA
draft. Despite the peculiar syntax, it was a welcoming sound.

Most acrimonious parting shot

*"I wouldn't give Charles Barkley an apology at gunpoint.
He can never expect an apology from me. If anything, he owes
me an apology for coming to play with his big fat butt."*
Scottie Pippen, Houston, October 1999

Pippen departed Houston and his beloved teammate,
Charles Barkley, shortly after delivering this ripping remark.

Most reckless reference to slavery

"We've got a lot of rebellious slaves on this team."
Larry Johnson, New York, June 22, 1999

Two days after Johnson was fined $25,000 for refusing to
make himself available to the media and then cursing
reporters and a league official during the 1999 finals, he
opened his mouth at a media session and would not stop
talking. The obscenity-filled diatribe, which touched on such
subjects as his parents, his critics, and his personal relation-
ships, lasted for 30 rambling minutes. Johnson's slave
remark, by which he meant that the Knicks were a team of
non-conformists, sounded hollow coming from a guy with
an $84-million contract.

Best endorsement for the beef industry

"I play my best ball at 345. I need my meat, because I'm going to take a beating. If you put a guy in front of me who eats salad and cucumber and baked chicken all day, I'll kill him."
Shaquille O'Neal, Miami, 2004

O'Neal would prefer that basketball eliminate scales and weight limits.

Most cosmic excuse for inconsistency

"It's beyond explanation. There are some things you can't understand—the Kennedy assassination, where the aliens are hiding, and our ups and downs. Oh, and Stonehenge."
Troy Murphy, Golden State, March 2003

The Warriors rookie began to get metaphysical when analyzing how his team could get blasted by Cleveland one night, then rebound to beat Boston the next.

Most black-and-white expression of frustration

"The one thing that always bothered me when I played in the NBA was I really got irritated when they put a white guy on me. I just didn't want a white guy guarding me. Because it's a disrespect to my game."
Larry Bird, June 2004

Bird caused a stir when he made this comment during an ESPN question-and-answer session.

Most black-and-white comment about race

"When you talk about race in basketball, the whole thing is simple: a black player knows he can go out on the court and kick a white player's ass."
Dennis Rodman

Rodman set fires wherever he went.

Best explanation for retiring

*"I knew it was time to retire when I was driving
the lane and got called for a three-second violation."*
Johnny "Red" Kerr, former NBA player and coach
There is slow and then there is really slow.

Best explanation for coming out of retirement

*"They said playing basketball would kill me. Well,
not playing basketball was killing me."*
Magic Johnson, Los Angeles, 1995
After retiring in 1991 because he had contracted HIV,
Johnson would subsequently make three returns to the
pumpkin patch.

Most prophetic quote by a Hall of Famer

*"I don't want to play 10 years in the NBA and
then die of a heart attack at age 40."*
Pete Maravich, Atlanta, 1974
Pistol Pete uttered this quote during a 1974 interview. In
an eerie coincidence, Maravich died of a heart attack in a
pickup basketball game in Pasadena, California, at age 40
on January 5, 1988. He had played 10 years in the NBA.
Maravich's last words before collapsing were, "I feel great."
An autopsy revealed that his death was due to a congenital
heart defect; he had been born with only one coronary artery
instead of the normal two.

[11]

BRANDED

Michael Jordan changed NBA player economics by transforming himself into a brand item. In 1992 *Forbes* magazine named Jordan the highest-paid athlete in the world, estimating his annual income at $35.9 million, of which only $3.9 million was derived from his player's salary.

Most successful athletic footware endorsement

"Air Jordans," Nike, Michael Jordan, 1985

Ironically, Jordan never wanted to sign with Nike. His first choice was Converse, the industry leader, whose endorsers included Larry Bird and Magic Johnson. But Converse wasn't interested in Jordan. Nike, only a bit player in basketball at the time, seized the opportunity and wooed Jordan by offering him his own signature model shoe. He eventually signed a deal for $500,000 that included a small cut of shoe revenues. When Nike released the first Air Jordan on April 1, 1985, it was estimated that perhaps 10,000 pairs would be sold by year's end. That total was a little on the low side. Retailers sold 450,000 pairs with a suggested price of $65 in less than a month. In Jordan's first full season under the Nike logo, the Air Jordan line generated $153 million in revenue. By 1997, Nike's worldwide sales had reached $9.2 billion.

First pro basketball player to endorse an athletic shoe

Julius Erving, Converse, 1976

Before there was Air Jordan there was Dr. J. The high-flying Erving not only revolutionized the game with his above-the-rim style, he was also the first pro basketball player to endorse a sneaker. Introduced in 1976, Converse's Dr. J's were white shoes adorned with a simple blue star and chevron. Produced in low-top and high-top styles, these "Limousines for the Feet" became a must-have for hoop-crazy kids.

First player fined for wearing colored basketball shoes
Michael Jordan, Chicago, 1985
The red-and-black Air Jordan sneaker that Nike introduced
in 1985 ran afoul of the NBA's "uniformity of uniforms" rule.
As a result, the league began fining Jordan $1,000 per game.
Even though his shoes matched the Bulls' team colors, NBA
rules stipulated that he could not wear shoes that were
different from those worn by his teammates. Nike turned
a potential marketing disaster into a triumph by creating
a commercial that tapped into the rebellious attitude of its
target audience. The ad copy went like this: "On October 14,
Nike created a revolutionary new basketball shoe. On October 18, the NBA threw them out of the game. Fortunately
the NBA can't keep you from wearing them. Air Jordans.
From Nike."

**First basketball shoe ad banned
for insulting a country's national dignity**
"Air Zoom LeBron II," Nike, November 2004
In 2004 Nike produced an animated TV commercial entitled
"Chamber of Fear" to hype its new line of LeBron James
endorsed sneakers, the Air Zoom LeBron II. The ad, which
featured a cartoon version of James battling and defending a
martial-arts expert, flying Oriental maidens, and dragons
made of smoke, struck a sore spot in Beijing. China banned
the ad, calling it "blasphemous" and an insult to China's
national dignity. Not wanting to offend its largest future
market, Nike apologized.

First basketball shoe recalled because it offended a religion
"Air Bakin'," Nike, 1997

Had Nike committed this design snafu in today's political
climate, its headquarters might have been car-bombed. As it
was, the shoe giant still came under considerable fire. The
controversy was sparked by Nike's new Air Bakin' shoe, or,
more specifically, the wavy graphic of the word Air on the
shoe's heel, which was engulfed in flames to convey the impression it was on fire. According to some Muslim clerics,
the graphic looked suspiciously like Arabic script for Allah,
or God. In the Muslim religion, any depiction of the word
Allah is treated with utmost respect, and because Muslims
consider feet and shoes to be unclean and lowly, the position-
ing of Nike's logo was especially offensive. In response to the
protests, Nike issued a public apology, recalled 38,000 pairs
of the shoe and made a $40,000 donation to a playground at
an Islamic elementary school.

Most influential TV ad campaign for a basketball shoe
Mars Blackmon and Michael Jordan, Nike, 1988

In 1988, the year that Jordan won his first MVP award, Nike
hired film director Spike Lee to shoot a series of TV ads promoting Jordan's basketball shoes. At the time, Nike's sales
had slumped from $1.1 billion to $877 million and the company had dropped to second in sneaker sales to Reebok. The
ads featured Lee playing a yappy bicycle messenger named
Mars Blackmon, who watched in awe as Jordan executed a
series of gravity defying dunks. "It's gotta be the shoes!"
declared Blackmon. The message—that people don't excel
at something because of practice and the right genes, but
simply because they have the right attitude and the right

shoes—was a master stroke. Sales rebounded to $1.2 billion in 1988, then boomed to $1.7 billion, $2.2 billion, and $3 billion in the next three years. The ad's creative momentum made Nike the most ubiquitous brand in sports, growing to a 43 percent market share in 1998 from 18 percent only 10 years earlier.

Most poorly timed player endorsement
LA Gear and Ron Artest, 2004
LA Gear, a young company trying to make a mark for itself in the sneaker business, did just that, but in all the wrong ways, when it signed Indiana's Ron Artest to endorse a new line of shoes and clothing in 2004. Just a couple of weeks into the LA Gear launch, Artest ignited a donnybrook in Detroit when he plunged into the stands in pursuit of a fan who had hit him with a cup of beer. The 72-game suspension that Artest received put the ad campaign in the deep freeze.

Most expensive basketball shoe
$65,000: Special Edition Iverson/Question, November 2004
The only question is why? In 2004, Reebok and jeweler Jacob Arabo teamed up to produce the ultimate in footwear decadence: a diamond-encrusted version of Allen Iverson's signature sneaker, "The Question." Made of sleek black leather with 246 diamonds set in pure white gold down each shoelace, the sneaker carried a price tag of $65,000.

Most money lost by canceling a shoe contract
$13.5 million: Vince Carter, Toronto, 2000
If the shoe doesn't fit, don't wear it. This is evidently Carter's motto and it cost him an arm and a leg. Prior to his rookie

season in 1998–99, the dunkmaster signed a $25-million dollar, five-year endorsement contract with Puma. The deal soon turned sour. Carter initially complained that the shoes did not fit him properly and hurt his feet; he later claimed that Puma failed in its obligation to him to make a signature shoe. Although no Puma shoe actually bore Carter's entire name, the company did introduce a black-and-white model known as "the Vinsanity" that was billed as "the favorite shoe worn on the court by Puma athlete and NBA superstar Vince Carter." The Raptors star stopped wearing Puma shoes and began wearing a different brand of sneaker nearly every game. Puma sued for breach of contract, arguing that Carter was trying to escape his deal to land a more lucrative arrangement with another manufacturer. An arbitrator ruled in favor of Puma and ordered Carter to pay $13.5 million in damages. The arbitrator also issued an injunction against Carter that prevented him from endorsing or wearing the footwear of any of Puma's competitors for three years. In September 2000 Carter signed a multi-year, $30-million endorsement deal with Nike. He used about half of that sum to settle his debt with Puma, including an extra $3 million to get the company to lift the injunction that stopped him from wearing another brand.

Age of youngest basketball player to endorse an athletic shoe
3: Mark Walker, Reebok, 2003

Welcome to the era of the three-year-old sneaker pimp. In September 2003 a basketball prodigy named Mark Walker became a Reebok endorser. "He's a threat from anywhere on the court," the company announced, "and he's only three-and-a-half years old." Reebok built an entire sales campaign around the basketball-playing tot and produced a television ad showing Walker sinking 18 shots in a row in his family garage. In another clip on Reebok's Web site, Walker tells the camera that his favorite foods are macaroni and hot dogs and that his favorite hoops stars are Allen Iverson and Kobe Bryant. The toddler's last comment is less cute. With wide, innocent eyes, he looks into the lens and says, "I am Reebok."

First lifetime shoe endorsement deal

Allen Iverson, Reebok, November 28, 2001

On June 26, 1996, Iverson was picked first overall by Philadelphia in the NBA draft. A couple of months later, the point guard signed a three-year, $9.4-million contract with the team. He also signed an even more lucrative 10-year, $50-million deal with Reebok. Iverson's signature shoe, "The Answer," quickly became Reebok's top-selling item. In November 2001, Iverson negotiated a contract extension on his initial deal with Reebok that will pay him an estimated $5 million a year for life. Although it's hard to grasp the logic behind a shoe manufacturer's decision to sign a pro athlete to a lifetime contract (especially one with as combustible a personality as Iverson's), the move seems to have launched a trend. In the wake of Iverson's ground-breaking deal, Tracy McGrady and Kevin Garnett inked lifetime endorsement contracts with Adidas.

Richest shoe endorsement by a basketball player

$90 million: LeBron James, Cleveland, May 21, 2003

There's no business like shoe business. A month before James was selected first overall by the Cleveland Cavaliers in the 2003 draft, the 18-year-old was already a multimillionaire.

James's sugar daddy was Nike, which outbid Reebok to sign the teen to a seven-year, $90-million endorsement package. How big a deal is that? Well, consider that Michael Jordan's original contract with Nike was worth a mere $2.5 million over five years. James's windfall is even more staggering when compared to other sports-endorsement pacts. It more than doubled a $40-million deal that Reebok inked with tennis star Venus Williams, and nearly doubled a $50-million arrangement between Reebok and Allen Iverson.

Largest two-week surge in stock prices caused by a basketball player
$3.8 billion: Michael Jordan, March, 1995
Jordan's 17-month retirement from basketball in the mid-1990s was not only bad for the NBA's bottom line, it also hurt the companies whose products he hyped. But that situation changed as rumors of the legend's impending return to the court gained speed. In a 12-day span from March 7, 1995, to Jordan's comeback on March 19, the stock of major public companies that he endorsed increased in market value by a combined $3.8 billion.

Most money lost in canceled endorsements, one season
$20 million plus: Kobe Bryant, Los Angeles, 2003–04
Before being charged in July 2003 with assaulting a 19-year-old woman at a Colorado resort, Bryant was one of the most popular sports celebrity pitchmen on the planet, with multimillion dollar endorsement deals with Nike, McDonald's, Sprite, Nutella, Upper Deck, and Spalding. After the details of his alleged sexual felony surfaced, McDonald's did not renew Bryant's three-year contract, which was valued at $20 million. Nutella, the makers of a

chocolate spread, dumped Bryant as well. Although the charges against Bryant were later dropped, the canceled endorsements cost him well over $20 million and left the status of his other endorsement deals in limbo.

First coach to trademark a slogan
Pat Riley, "Threepeat," Los Angeles, 1988
After the Los Angeles Lakers won their second straight NBA title in 1988, coach Pat Riley and guard Byron Scott held a brainstorming session to come up with a phrase to motivate the team for another run at the title. The result, "Threepeat," soon appeared on shirts and hats around Los Angeles and made a small fortune for one of its creators. Though Scott did most of the thinking, he later explained that Riley "did a good job of making sure he patented it." The Detroit Pistons spoiled L.A.'s bid for a third consecutive title in the 1989 finals, but when the Chicago Bulls later achieved the feat of winning three straight championships in 1993 and then again in 1998, anyone who tried to make a buck selling Threepeat T-shirts had to pay Riley royalties. All told, Riley is estimated to have made about a million dollars on the slogan.

First player to have his own spokespuppet
Penny Hardaway, Li'l Penny, mid-1990s
A 14-inch spokespuppet featuring the voice of comedian Chris Rock was created to promote a line of Nike shoes endorsed by Orlando Magic guard Penny Hardaway in the mid-1990s. Li'l Penny's hysterical, trash-talking TV ads and his signature phrase, "Could ya do that for a brotha?" made the puppet an overnight celebrity. The mechanical doll

would make an appearance on *The Oprah Winfrey Show* and publish his autobiography, *Knee High and Livin' Large,* written with Stacy Wall. His commercials, however, were the highlight of his short-lived career. The most unforgettable spots included LP and Spike Lee courtside at a Magic-Knicks game, Penny and Nick Anderson promoting Ken Griffey for president, and one in which LP is seen blowing bubbles, launching rockets, and hanging with Tyra Banks as Hardaway and others played street ball. Unfortunately for Li'l Penny, his showbiz career fizzled when Hardaway's skills went into sudden decline.

First player to endorse his own cologne

Michael Jordan, Chicago, 1996

Ah, yes, the fresh smell of money. Michael Jordan Cologne, designed by Bijon Fragrances, was unveiled at a promotion on September 25, 1996, in Culver City, California, by Jordan himself. A few weeks later, the hoopster appeared on *Larry King Live* to plug his line of musk. Jordan brought along four tiny vials, each containing an essence that supposedly captured an aspect of his character: Cool, Home Run, Pebble Beach, and Rare Air. Cool exuded the woodsy bouquet of Jordan's home state of North Carolina; Home Run smelled of leather; Pebble Beach was redolent of grass. Jordan described the aroma of Rare Air as "Powerful and mysterious. The sense of being able to walk away from something you have mastered and strive to prove yourself in another arena." The description blended ad-copy patter with his oft-repeated explanation of why he suddenly quit the NBA in 1993 and took up baseball. Sadly, Jordan was serious.

First player to become a Celebriduck

Allen Iverson, Philadelphia, January 2001

In the late 1990s an entrepreneur named Craig Wolfe began producing collectible rubber ducks imprinted with the faces of celebrities such as Groucho Marx, Shakespeare, Betty Boop, and James Brown (who insisted his duck appear in a green suit). Celebriducks made their professional sports debut at a Philadelphia 76ers game on January 11, 2001, when 5,500 Allen Iverson models—replete with cornrows, tattoos, and a black elbow sleeve—were given away. According to 76ers executive vice-president Dave Coskey, Iverson had no objections to the daffy transformation. "Allen thought we were nuts anyway by then, but when I showed him a prototype of the duck, he smirked and said, 'It's crazy,' but he approved it." The company has since produced Celebriducks of a dozen other NBA stars including Kobe Bryant, Tim Duncan, Vince Carter, and Latrell Sprewell.

First player to create his own sports drink

Lebron James, Cleveland, 2004

James possesses more talents than anyone realized. The NBA's 2004 Rookie of the Year is also a soft-drink chemist. According to an August 2004 Coca-Cola press release, James was involved in every aspect of the creation of Powerade FLAVA23, from choosing its "sourberry" flavor, to selecting the drink's burgundy color and developing the package graphics, which feature a stylized image of James soaring through the air. James's deal with the Powerade and Sprite brands is worth about $2 million a year, but there are incentives in his contract that will boost that sum if his endorsement leads to greater sales. Powerade could use the help, since its share of the market is 15 percent, compared with the 81 percent share enjoyed by Gatorade.

First player to endorse a tire with his hair

Richard "Rip" Hamilton, Detroit, January 2005

NBA players aren't allowed to use their uniforms for advertising, so Detroit Pistons guard Rip Hamilton used his head. Goodyear Tire and Rubber Company paid Hamilton to wear his tightly braided hair in the style of the tread pattern of the company's Assurance TripleTred product. "The way he plays fits nicely with the product: confident maneuvering, handles well in all conditions," said company spokesman Ed Markey. Hamilton debuted his new do in a game against the New York Knicks on January 29, 2005. That same week he also sported the cut at the White House when President George W. Bush hosted the Pistons at a reception in honor of their 2004 NBA championship.

First player to buy his own record label

Chris Webber, Washington, 1996

Webber bought his own rap label, Humility Records, in 1996. The purchase caused Webber to add a new wrinkle to his on-court theatrics. Whenever he made a big scoring play, he would form a triangle symbol with his hands. Washington fans were initially mystified by the gesture, but it was later revealed that Webber was simply trying to get some free publicity—the shape was supposed to represent the logo of his record label.

First player to sell a million copies of a rap album
Shaquille O'Neal, Orlando, 1993
"Every basketball player wants to be a rapper and every rap-per wants to be a basketball player," O'Neal once stated. The giant center fulfilled both ambitions in 1993 when he released his first CD, entitled "Shaq Diesel." Recorded with the help of O'Neal's favorite group, Fu-Schnickens, the album featured such tunes as "I Hate 2 Brag," "Shoot Pass Slam," and "Where You At?" Not everyone was impressed with O'Neal's musical gifts, but the album sold more than a million copies. Since then, he has released several more CDs.

First player to record a rap song with a supermodel
Kobe Bryant, Los Angeles, 2000
In a fit of lunacy, Columbia Records released a rap duet by Bryant and supermodel Tyra Banks in 2000. The song, enti-tled, "K.O.B.E.," featured the busty Banks crooning "K-O-B-E, I L-O-V-E you." In response, Kobe rapped, "Uh, what I live for? Basketball, beats, and broads." The track was recorded for a Bryant CD entitled "Visions," which was deemed so terrible that Columbia never released it.

First player reprimanded for his rap lyrics
Allen Iverson, Philadelphia, October 2000
Iverson's initial foray into the recording business hit the headlines. His rap single "40 Barz" featured such heart-warming lyrics as "Come to me with those faggot tendencies and you'll be sleeping with the maggots be"; and "Get money, kill and fuckin' bitches, I'm hittin' anything and planning on using my riches"; and "Man enough to pull a gun, be man enough to squeeze it." The song ends with the

sound of a revolver being cocked and fired. Iverson defended the violent imagery and angry messages in "40 Barz" by going on the offensive. "If your kid goes out and blows somebody's head off because Allen Iverson has said he was going to blow somebody's head off on wax, then you're doing a bad job as a parent." After a meeting with NBA commissioner David Stern, who described the lyrics as "coarse, offensive, and anti-social," Iverson agreed to eliminate the most offensive words from the final version of his album, which was entitled, with no sense of irony, "Non-Fiction." The album was never released.

First player benched for asking for time off to promote a rap album
Ron Artest, Indiana, November 2004
Artest considers himself a "true warrior." In fact, that's the title he chose for his record label, Tru Warier. So how's this for the warrior spirit? Early in the 2004–05 season, Artest went to coach Rick Carlisle and asked for a month off to rest his tired body and to allow him to handle some promo work for his fledgling record label. The 24-year-old power forward was scheduled to release his debut rap album later in the month. "I've been doing a little bit too much music, just needed the rest," Artest explained. "After the album comes out I'm going to make sure all of my time is focused on winning a championship." Carlisle responded by benching Artest for two games, saying he had "compromised the integrity of the team." When asked by reporters for his take on his coach's criticism, Artest said he didn't know what the word "integrity" meant. A week later, Artest got his time off when his role in an ugly brawl with fans earned him a season-long suspension.

[12]

MEN
IN SUITS

If Armani-clad Pat Riley wins the award for best-dressed NBA coach, then Doug Moe takes the trophy for the worst dressed. The sloppily attired Moe once said: "My only rule is that you have to dress better than me to be acceptable." In this chapter the guys who normally walk the sidelines take the floor.

Fastest firing of a coach

1 game: Dolph Schayes, Buffalo, 1971–72

It didn't take the Buffalo Braves long to decide that Schayes was not their man. He was gone after Buffalo lost its 1971–72 home opener to the Atlanta Hawks. The previous year, Schayes coached the expansion Braves to a 22–60 record. Under his replacement, John McCarthy, they went 21–60.

Most coaching jobs lost by punching an owner, one week

2: Jim Harding, Minnesota Pipers (ABA), January 1969

Harding was set to coach the Eastern Division in the ABA All-Star game on January 28, 1969, when, on the night before the event, he became embroiled in a fistfight with Gabe Rubin, one of the Pipers owners. ABA commissioner George Mikan relieved Harding of his All-Star duties and two days later Harding was fired by the Pipers, making him a perfect two-for-one for the week.

Only coach to punch out an opposition owner during the pre-game warm-up

Red Auerbach, Boston, April 6, 1957

A dispute over the height of the basket at Kiel Auditorium before Game 3 of the 1957 NBA finals led to a confrontation between Celtics coach Red Auerbach and Hawks owner Ben Kerner. When Kerner began screaming obscenities at Auerbach, the Boston coach decked him at midcourt in front of a sold-out crowd. Kerner, who suffered a bloody nose, was escorted back to his seat while Auerbach returned to the Boston bench and the game proceeded. Auerbach was fined $300 for the punch. If the move was designed to fire his team up, it failed to work. St. Louis won 100–98.

Only coach to lose his job because of a bicycle accident

Jack McKinney, Los Angeles, November 1979

Fourteen games into the 1979–80 season, McKinney suffered
a serious head injury in a bicycle accident. He had been
headed to a tennis match with his best friend and Lakers assistant coach, Paul Westhead, when the crash occurred. For a
time, it appeared McKinney might not survive. At the very
least, he was faced with months of convalescence; so Westhead took over as interim coach. The position became a permanent one when the Lakers rolled to first in the West and
went on to capture the NBA title. Fully recovered from his
injuries, McKinney was hired by the Indiana Pacers the following year, where he won Coach of the Year honors.

Most cigars smoked by a coach during games, career

Several hundred: Red Auerbach, 1946–47 *to* 1965–66

Fidel Castro, Winston Churchill, and George Burns may rank
as the world's most famous cigar smokers, but Auerbach is
the king of the sports world. He liked to fire up a fat stogie
on the bench during the final minutes of NBA games when
his team had the victory well in hand. Considering that Auerbach coached the Boston Celtics to nine NBA championships,
he had plenty of opportunities to blow smoke up the opposition's ass. The fact that Auerbach lit up before the game was
over struck many as arrogant, though he viewed it differently.
Auerbach believed that casually puffing on a cigar when your
team is far ahead was more sportsmanlike than aggressively
pushing your team to pad the score. As he once said: "You got
a team by 30 points, there's three minutes to go. The coach is
still pacing up and down the sidelines and yelling. For what?
He's on TV. He wants to show that his team fights and is

active for the full 48 minutes and he's an integral part of it. My feeling was that once the game is decided—and you could tell—then sit down and relax." Tempting as it may be, no other coach will ever copy Auerbach's trademark gesture, or threaten his unofficial record. Since smoking is now prohibited in NBA arenas, the victory cigar has become an indulgence reserved for postgame celebrations.

Most memorable pre-game assist by a coach

Maurice Cheeks, Portland, April 25, 2003

Cheeks chalked up 7,392 assists in 16 NBA seasons before becoming Portland's coach in 2001, but his best assist was the one he gave to 13-year-old Natalie Gilbert on April 25, 2003. Prior to Game 3 of the Mavericks-Blazers playoff series in Portland, Gilbert began to sing "The Star-Spangled Banner" before a crowd of nearly 20,000. But overcome with stage fright she faltered and forgot the words and was left nervously shaking until Cheeks walked over from his team's bench, put his arm around the girl, and began to sing with her. Gilbert got back on track and the packed house, the players, and the duo finished the song together. As they waked off the court, Cheeks told her, "Don't worry kid. Everyone has a bad game once in awhile."

First coach to leave a game for a sandwich

Frank Layden, Utah, March 12, 1985

Extreme hunger or extreme disinterest? The Utah Jazz were being thumped by the Los Angeles Lakers. By the fourth quarter it was clear that Utah had no chance; the score was 123–108 and the Lakers were dominating play at both ends of the court. Utah's head coach, 300-pound Frank Layden, decided he had seen enough. He turned control of the team over to his assistant, left the arena, and went to a nearby deli to grab a snack.

First coach suspended for allowing another team to break a record
Doug Moe, Denver, November 22, 1983
Trailing badly in a 1983 game against Portland and with the Trail Blazers nearing a single-game scoring record of 150 points, Moe called a time-out with 1:12 left. But instead of trying to rally his troops, Moe told his players: "Let them have it. You understand what I am saying don't you?" The Nuggets let the Blazers score five uncontested baskets for a 156–116 win. Moe was fined $5,000 and suspended for two games.

Most games won without underwear, one season
64: George Karl, Seattle, 1995–96
Fruit of the Loom has not made any money off Karl. "I coach every game out there free and loose [without underwear]," Karl confessed in an April 2002 *Esquire* interview. "There's an old cliché in coaching: when there's a tight situation, grab your left ball. I've done that. Anything to help." The briefless Karl coached Seattle to the finals in 1995–96.

Most consecutive wins from the start of a career
13: Lawrence Frank, New Jersey, 2003–04
Who is Lawrence Frank? That's what everyone was asking in February 2004 after Frank began his NBA coaching career in record-setting style, guiding New Jersey to a 13–0 mark from January 27 to February 24. The 13-game winning streak not only set a new NBA mark for most consecutive

wins by a coach to begin a career, it was also the longest winning streak of any coach in any of the four major professional sports to begin a career. Frank, who had never been a head coach at any level, was only supposed to be an interim replacement until the Nets found someone better. After the streak ended, the Nets went 25–15 the rest of the way and Frank was hired as head coach.

Most consecutive losses from the start of a career
17: Ron Rothstein, Miami, 1988–89
Rothstein had the thankless task of coaching the expansion Miami Heat in its inaugural season. Before the year began he joked, "I have a great lawyer who negotiated my contract—it says I can't be fired until the team has three wins." Rothstein needed a sense of humor. Miami lost its first 17 games, an NBA record for futility, and finished the campaign with a 15–67 record.

Most consecutive 50-win seasons from the start of a career
13: Pat Riley, 1981–82 to 1994–95
No one has been so successful so quickly and for so long as Riley. He took over in Los Angeles early in 1981–82 when head coach Paul Westhead was fired after a dispute with superstar Magic Johnson over strategy. Riley installed the fast-breaking offensive style that Johnson desired and reaped the benefits when the club posted nine straight 50-win seasons and won four championships. After taking a year off in 1990–91 Riley relocated to New York and piloted the Knicks to four consecutive 50-win seasons before moving to Miami in 1995, where he experienced the first mediocre season of his career with the 42–40 Heat.

Most consecutive wins from the start of a season

15: Red Auerbach, Washington, November 3 to December 4, 1948
15: Rudy Tomjanovich, Houston, November 5 to December 2, 1993
The two fastest NBA teams out of the chute came to very
different ends. Auerbach's Capitols hit a wall in 1948–49
after winning 15 straight and ended with a 38–20 mark.
The Capitols were beaten by Minneapolis in the finals and
Auerbach was fired. Tomjanovich's Rockets also slowed
down after their fast start in 1993–94, finishing with a
58–24 record, but regained their momentum in the playoffs
and won the NBA title.

Most consecutive wins, one season

33: Bill Sharman, Los Angeles, 1971–72
Sharman replaced Joe Mullaney as Lakers coach in the fall
of 1971. It didn't take him long to get results. After nine
games, the Lakers' record stood at six wins and three losses.
The club then proceeded to reel off an incredible 33 straight
victories. During the streak the Lakers were rarely even seriously tested; they played only one overtime game during the
span and their smallest margin of victory was four points, in
the first game of the streak against Baltimore. The run finally
ended in Milwaukee on January 9, 1972, when the Bucks
stomped L.A. 120–104.

Most consecutive losses, one season

23: Brian Winters, Vancouver, 1995–96
23: Bill Hanzlik, Denver, 1997–98
Winters has found himself in a hellish situation twice in
his coaching career. He was the first coach of the toothless
Vancouver Grizzlies team that set the NBA futility record

by losing 23 straight games in the 1995–96 campaign. The Grizzlies had that dubious record all to themselves until 1997–98 when the hapless Denver Nuggets, coached by Bill Hanzlik and assisted by Winters, dropped 23 in a row.

Most consecutive road losses

43: Dick Motta, Sacramento, November 21, 1990,
to November 22, 1991

Motta's three-year stint in Sacramento was a train wreck from start to finish. He clashed with his young players, failed to inspire the veterans, and the team went nowhere despite a league-record four first-round draft picks in 1990. But worst of all was the Kings' horrifying road record. The travel-phobic club lost 43 consecutive games on the road over two seasons before it finally broke the jinx on November 23, 1991, by squeaking past Orlando 95–93. The win came as such a relief that Motta had the team bus pull into a con-venience store after the game where he bought everyone six-packs. A month later Motta was fired on Christmas Eve. He called it "the best Christmas present I ever had."

Most wins by a replacement coach, one season

50: Paul Westhead, Los Angeles, 1979–80
50: Pat Riley, Los Angeles, 1981–82

Two Lakers rookie coaches, just two years apart, share this mark. Assistant coach Westhead replaced Jack McKinney after he was injured in a bicycling accident after 14 games and guided the Lakers to a 50–18 mark the rest of the way, eventually winning the title, thanks to the inspired play of rookie guard Magic Johnson. But after the Lakers came up short the next season, Westhead attempted to restructure the offense in a way that Johnson believed would have reduced his role. Eleven games into the 1981–82 season, Johnson exploded in the locker room after a game in Utah. "I can't play here anymore. I want to leave. I want to be traded." Westhead was fired the next day and replaced by assistant coach Pat Riley. At Riley's first home game, fans at the Forum booed Johnson during the introductions. In Seattle he was jeered whenever he touched the ball. But Johnson silenced the hecklers by carrying the team to another title, as the Lakers went 50–21 under Riley to match Westhead's record.

Most dramatic impact by a replacement coach
Lenny Wilkens, Seattle, 1977–78
Before the 1972–73 season, Seattle's management told 35-year-old playing-coach Lenny Wilkens to lose one of the hats he was wearing. Wilkens opted to keep playing and Seattle hired Tom Nissalke as its new bench boss. To assert his control, Nissalke promptly traded Wilkens to Cleveland. Five years later, Wilkens was brought back by the Sonics as director of player personnel. But when Seattle stumbled in the early going, the club gassed coach Bob Hopkins and gave Wilkens the job. At that point, the team was in the cellar with a 5–17 record. The Sonics took off, winning 18 of their next 21 games and going 42–18 the rest of the way. Wilkens's magic carried Seattle through to the 1978 NBA finals, where the Sonics lost in seven games to Washington. Next season, he coached Seattle to the crown.

Longest span between Coach of the Year awards

26 years: Hubie Brown, 1977–78 to 2003–04

The granddaddy of coaches, Brown coached in the pros for 33 years, 15 of them in the NBA. He first won the Coach of the Year award with the Atlanta Hawks in 1977–78. He won his second award in 2003–04 when he turned around a dead-beat Grizzlies franchise, getting 50 wins out of a team that had suffered 54 losses the year before. Brown was 70 years old at the time.

Only coach to win a Coach of the Year award with a losing team

Johnny "Red" Kerr, Chicago, 1966–67

The voters for the Coach of the Year award clearly prefer the underdog. Coaches of great teams don't get the same credit. How else to explain the decision to give Kerr the award in 1966–67 instead of Philadelphia's Alex Hannum? All Hannum did in his first year with the 76ers was lead his team to a franchise-record 68 wins and an NBA championship. Kerr's work with the expansion Bulls was considered better because his team wasn't nearly as bad as everyone expected. The Bulls finished with a 33–48 record, but made the playoffs.

Most wins by a rookie coach, one season

62: Paul Westphal, Phoenix, 1992–93

Westphal parachuted into Phoenix at an opportune time. The team was just moving into brand new America West Arena and had made a tasty off-season trade, acquiring Charles Barkley from Philadelphia. The Suns amassed a league-high 62 wins under their rookie bench boss and advanced to the finals where they were beaten by Chicago in six games.

Most losses by a rookie coach, one season

71: Bill Hanzlik, Denver, 1997–98

Hiring Hanzlik was a mistake. The Nuggets players could never fully grasp the system he wanted to install and the result was a nightmarish 11–71 season. The 71 losses also happens to be the record for most by any coach in a single NBA season. A couple of other teams have lost more games in a season, but they did not stick with the same coach for the entire debacle.

First NBA coach to inspire a movie character

Pat Riley, Los Angeles, 1987

Despite his incredible success as a coach, Riley may be best remembered for his hair. His glistening, slick-backed look was copied by actor Michael Douglas when he played the role of stockbroker Gordon Gekko in the 1987 film *Wall Street*. Douglas's chilling portrayal of the driven and manipulative Gekko was said to be based on more of Riley than simply his hair. It won Douglas an Academy Award for Best Actor.

Strangest car accident involving a coach

Jeff Van Gundy, New York, May 18, 2000

We are all familiar with the phrase "hang time"—but with a Honda Civic? After the Knicks flew home from a 2000 play-off game in Miami, their cars were driven out onto the tarmac at Westchester County Airport so the players and staff could head home. But before they had a chance to get in their vehicles, the chartered jet turned to move down the runway. As the plane taxied forward, the pilot revved one of the engines. The jet's discharge caught Van Gundy's 1995 Honda Civic and sent it airborne. The vehicle sailed through the air and smashed into guard Allan Houston's 1997 Mercedes, assistant coach Brendan Malone's 1999 Lincoln, and the team media-relations director's car, doing serious damage to all three. Van Gundy's Civic was totally demolished.

Strangest motivational technique used by a coach

Spliced movies: Phil Jackson

Jackson, the Zen master, is known for his novel motivational techniques, such as having his players practice meditation or giving them reading assignments (he once asked Shaquille O'Neal to read Nietzsche), but none was any odder than his use of audiovisual aids. During the Chicago Bulls' first championship playoff run, for example, he intercut film sequences of the club's game footage with scenes from *The Wizard of Oz*. Like the Wizard, Jackson was trying to make his players realize that the heart, courage, and brains they needed lay latent within them. In the 2000 playoffs he lifted scenes from *American History X* to prepare for a series with the Sacramento Kings. Jackson wanted to use the film and its underlying message of the brotherhood of man to unite his feuding stars, Kobe Bryant and Shaquille O'Neal. But he also took things in a very different direction by cutting back and forth between actor Edward Norton's menacing character, who has a bald head and a swastika tattoo, and Sacramento's shaven-headed and tattooed point guard, Jason Williams. Jackson also juxtaposed shots of Sacramento coach Rick Adelman, who has a mustache and distinctly German features, with Adolf Hitler. Presumably the message was that the Kings were the bad guys. The Lakers got the point, beating Sacramento in five games.

First coach to sue an opposition player

Butch Carter, Toronto, April 21, 2000

Two days before the Raptors and Knicks opened their 2000 playoff series, Carter filed a $5-million defamation lawsuit against the Knicks Marcus Camby, after the former Toronto forward called him a "liar" and said many players didn't like him. Camby claimed he had been traded to the Knicks just days after Carter promised to build the Raptors around him. After a talk with NBA deputy commissioner Russ Granik, Carter admitted he was wrong to sue Camby. "Bringing the courthouse into the locker room was not the best way to address this particular matter."

First coach fined for making a racist remark

John Calipari, New Jersey, March 1997

Calipari flipped out when reporter Dan Garcia of the *Newark Star-Ledger* wrote some critical remarks about his coaching acumen and gave him a "D" on a mid-season report card. Calipari confronted Garcia, who had covered the Nets for nine years, in a parking lot after a practice, called him a "fucking Mexican idiot" and threatened to punch him in the face. When Garcia reported the incident to the league, Calipari began backpedaling. "I would like to apologize to Dan Garcia for my ill-advised attempt at humor and insensitivity for the remark," he said in a statement. "In retrospect, I can understand how the remark could have been misinterpreted. I am sorry for any pain my remarks have caused." It was unclear exactly how Calipari's remarks could have been misinterpreted. After NBA commissioner David Stern assessed Calipari a $25,000 fine, Garcia sued the Nets coach, contending that he suffered "extreme humiliation and emotional distress" as a result of the insult. The lawsuit followed the breakdown of negotiations between Garcia and the Nets, in which Garcia had requested a hefty monetary settlement. A judge later dismissed the lawsuit, stating that it did not have any legal merit.

First coach to resign for making a "racially insensitive" remark
Dan Issel, Denver, December 26, 2001
Initially, Issel, the president and head coach of the Denver Nuggets, was suspended four games for shouting a profanity and an "insensitive racial remark" after a tough loss to the Charlotte Hornets on December 11, 2001. While leaving the court Issel berated a heckler, saying, "Hey, go drink another beer, you fucking Mexican piece of shit." The local NBC affiliate, KUSA, captured the incident on tape. The four-game suspension cost Issel $112,000. He publicly apologized at a press conference, and NBA commissioner David Stern announced that Issell would face no further disciplinary action. But the issue wasn't dead. Denver Hispanic Chamber of Commerce President Victoria Barela called the four-game suspension "completely laughable," and local Hispanic activists began boycotting Denver's games in a campaign to have Issel fired. Under mounting pressure, he resigned two weeks later.

Only coach assessed a technical foul for fainting
Jerry Reynolds, Sacramento, December 27, 1988
Reynolds had a reputation for pulling pranks, so when he collapsed to the floor during a game against Portland, every-one thought he was just fooling around. The referee even called a technical foul against Reynolds because he thought

the coach was mocking his calls. It took awhile for everyone to realize that Reynolds wasn't joking: he had passed out in front of the Kings bench. Help was quickly summoned and the coach was revived and rushed to a nearby hospital. Luckily, medical tests detected no problem.

Most pathetic attempt by a coach to break up a fight
Jeff Van Gundy, New York, April 30, 1998
In the final seconds of Game 4 of the New York–Miami 1998 playoff series, the Heat's Alonzo Mourning and the Knicks' Larry Johnson got into a shoving match. New York's diminutive coach, Jeff Van Gundy, rushed in to quell the melee but the best he could do was grab onto Mourning's leg. As the players shoved and wrestled, Van Gundy was dragged around the court like a rag doll. The coach got kicked a few times and stepped on, and admitted the next day that he knew he "looked like a fool." But, he said, "I don't regret going out there. I was trying to protect my player. Whether it was appropriate or not, I'll let everybody else judge."

First coach to guarantee a repeat championship
Pat Riley, Los Angeles, June 1987
At the party following the club's 1987 title, Lakers coach Pat Riley boldly guaranteed—not predicted, but guaranteed—a repeat championship in 1988, a feat that had not been accomplished in 18 years. "Guaranteeing a championship was the best thing Pat ever did," said Lakers guard Byron Scott. "It set the stage in our minds. Work harder, be better. That's the only way we could repeat." The Lakers delivered, but just barely, surviving three straight seven-game playoff series against Utah, Dallas, and Detroit.

Last player-coach

Lenny Wilkens, Portland, 1974–75

It's fitting that the man who has coached the most NBA games is also the NBA's last player-coach. Wilkens appeared in 16 games for Portland in 1974–75, averaging about 18 minutes per game. The Trail Blazers finished at 38–44 and missed the playoffs.

Last player-coach to win a championship

Bill Russell, Boston, 1969

After the Boston Celtics wrapped up the 1966 finals, coach Red Auerbach announced he was handing over the reins to Bill Russell, the team's heart and soul, who would serve as player-coach. The hiring made Russell the first black head coach in any major sport. In his first season at the helm, the Celtics' eight-year title streak ended with a loss in the Eastern finals to Wilt Chamberlain and the 76ers. But Boston rebounded in 1968, beating the Lakers in the finals. In 1969 Russell, who at age 35 still ranked third in the league in rebounding (19.3) but averaged a career-low 9.9 points, wasn't the same force on the court he had once been, but his will to win was undimmed. The Celtics, who finished fourth in the East, pulled off three playoff upsets, culminating with a gritty Game 7 triumph over the Lakers in Los Angeles to give Russell his 11th NBA title in 13 years. Two months later he retired.

[13]

MEDIA MADNESS

Legendary Boston Celtics announcer Johnny Most was an excitable type. During one game he nearly lost his dentures over the rail of the upper press deck. On another memorable occasion, the chain smoker gave new meaning to the term "hot pants" when he accidentally set fire to his trousers during a broadcast.

First player to claim he was misquoted in his autobiography

Charles Barkley, Philadelphia, 1992

Barkley was quoted in his 1992 autobiography, *Outrageous!: The Fine Life and Flagrant Good Times of Basketball's Irresistible Force,* as saying that 76ers teammate Armon Gilliam was not a consistent scorer or rebounder and that giving up a No. 1 draft pick to get Manute Bol was a dumb move. An outraged Barkley complained that he had never said any such thing about either of his teammates. When it was pointed out that the statements came from his own book, he backtracked. "That was my fault. I should have read it before it came out."

Strangest attire worn by a player for a book launch

A bridal gown: Dennis Rodman, Chicago, August 21, 1996

On a late summer afternoon in New York City, Rodman pulled up to the Barnes & Noble bookstore on Fifth Avenue in a horse-drawn carriage, fully decked out in a wedding dress, feather boa, and blond wig, trailed by a cortege of tuxedo-clad women. On the *David Letterman Show* the previous night, the 35-year-old Chicago Bulls player had told America he'd exchange vows the next day with a "beautiful and intelligent woman," but the following afternoon, there was no bride (or groom, for that matter) in sight. The man who had apparently married himself then sat down beneath a mural depicting such literary heavyweights as Ernest Hemingway and James Joyce and signed copies of his first book, *Bad As I Wanna Be.* This garish display of androgyny landed Rodman on Mr. Blackwell's list of the worst-dressed women of 1996 and helped generate a blizzard of publicity that propelled his book up the best-seller list.

Best-selling self-help book written by a Hall of Famer

The Memory Book: Jerry Lucas, 1974

The only forward to haul down 40 boards in an NBA game, the six-foot-eight Lucas attributed his rebounding skill to the powers of the mind. He would memorize the angles that balls rebounded off a backboard so he could anticipate their direction. When his career ended, Lucas found new ways to make money with his memory. In the early 1970s he appeared on television and amazed a national audience with his ability to memorize the first 500 pages of the Manhattan phone directory. In 1974 Lucas co-authored *The Memory Book,* a how-to bestseller that sold more than two million copies. In the late 1980s, he established Lucas Learning Inc., an educational company that published memory and learning materials for children. In all, the former rebound king has written more than 30 books on the subject.

Most expensive penalty for the use of a curse word

$295,000: Shaquille O'Neal, Los Angeles, February 2004

O'Neal was suspended for one game without pay by the NBA for using obscene language and criticizing the officials during a television interview after an 84–83 Lakers win over the Toronto Raptors in 2004. He later apologized, but the suspension cost him $295,000. "I said what I felt," O'Neal admitted. "You can never control me. I'm a 31-year-old juvenile delinquent. No one can control me."

Largest fine for insulting a religion in a postgame interview

$50,000: Dennis Rodman, Chicago, June 1997

After Game 3 of the 1997 finals against the Jazz in Salt Lake City, Rodman explained his poor play by saying, "It's

difficult to get in sync because of all the Mormons out here,"
inserting an expletive to describe the religious group. Those
and other disparaging remarks led to a $50,000 fine from the
NBA and public criticism from the NAACP and the Anti-
Defamation League. Rodman later offered an apology, claiming he was upset with Jazz fans and not the Mormon
religion. "As far as people who go to games and give me the
finger, I think that's wrong. They call me a lot of names, the
people in the stands. As far as the religion, I have no business
saying anything like that, so I take that statement back."
Bulls coach Phil Jackson argued that Rodman's only crime
was ignorance. "To Dennis, a Mormon may just be a nickname for people from Utah. He may not even know it's a
religious cult or sect or whatever it is," said Jackson.

Largest fine for uttering a cliché

$10,000: *Rasheed Wallace, Portland, April 2003*
Wallace stopped talking to reporters during the first three
games of Portland's 2003 playoff series with Dallas. When
coach Maurice Cheeks was asked why his forward had gone
silent, he twisted himself into a pretzel trying to take both
sides of the issue. "He doesn't really want to talk to the press,
for whatever reason. I don't condone his actions, and I'm not
saying its right or wrong." The NBA, however, which takes
its media image very seriously, threatened to fine Wallace if
he didn't open his mouth. So he complied, sort of. After
Portland's victory in Game 4, Wallace answered every question from reporters the same way. "It was a great game. Both
teams played hard." The league was not amused. It fined
Wallace $10,000 for lack of media cooperation. He was then
fined another $20,000 for not attending the interview session

after the next day's practice. Portland was also fined $50,000—$25,000 for each of Wallace's transgressions.

Largest fine for refusing to wear a microphone
$100,000: Seattle and Toronto, March 13, 2000
"Is this thing on?" The NBA thought that putting wireless mikes on coaches during games would be an innovative move. Just one problem: the coaches didn't agree. In fact, they hated the idea. Paul Westphal of Seattle and Butch Carter of Toronto rebuffed a league directive to wear clip-on microphones during a nationally televised game in March 2000. In response, the league fined their teams $100,000 each. The NBA had been looking for a new gimmick to boost TV ratings, which had declined dramatically after the lock-out-shortened 1998–99 season, and it had hoped that mik-ing coaches during games to tap into conversations with players and others would spark viewer interest. But West-phal contended that wearing a microphone would hamper his ability to coach. He was also worried that his instructions to his players could be intercepted by other teams. When other coaches protested, the league dropped the idea and rescinded the fines.

Most controversial business observation by an NBA owner
Scandal is good for the NBA: Mark Cuban,
Dallas, August 4, 2003
When Lakers star Kobe Bryant was charged with sexually assaulting a 19-year-old Colorado hotel employee in July 2003, most people reacted with shock and dismay. Bryant's career had been unblemished by scandal and it seemed to be a serious blow to the league. But Mark Cuban, the outspoken

Dallas Mavericks owner, saw it differently. In an interview with *Access Hollywood,* he stated: "From a business perspective, it's great for the NBA. It's reality television, people love train wreck television and you hate to admit it, but that is the truth, that's the reality today." Cuban also noted, "I would expect the first Lakers game to draw the biggest ratings for a regular-season game in a long, long time." NBA commissioner David Stern delivered a sharp rebuke to Cuban. "Any suggestion that there will be some economic or promotional benefit to the NBA arising from the charge pending against Kobe Bryant is both misinformed and unseemly." But Cuban's prediction proved accurate. There were two NBA games broadcast on Turner Network Television on opening night. The first—between the Phoenix Suns and the Orlando Magic—netted a 2.4 rating, while the second—between Cuban's Mavericks and Bryant's Lakers—scored a 3.0 rating. Together, the two games delivered 2.3 million households, the largest opening-night audience in the history of the NBA on TNT. Ironically, Bryant, the man in the eye of the media hurricane, did not play—reportedly due to a sore knee.

Most minutes of a playoff telecast pre-empted by a car chase
41: New York vs. Houston, June 17, 1994
NBC's telecast of Game 5 of the 1994 NBA finals between the New York Knicks and Houston Rockets suddenly vanished from the screen, replaced instead by an overhead shot of a white Ford Bronco cruising down a Los Angeles freeway, pursued by a convoy of police cars. Inside the Bronco was O.J. Simpson, the prime suspect in the murder of his wife, Nicole, just a few days before. Simpson had a gun held to his head, while his best friend, Al Cowlings, sat in the other seat

trying to persuade him not to pull the trigger. The players at the game knew what was going on, because the television sets at the arena kept cutting to the chase during time-outs. As Robert Horry of the Rockets recalled, "When we got into the locker room at halftime, [head coach] Rudy T was giving us our usual talk, going over strategy and plans. But the TV was on behind him, and you could see all of the guys weren't even paying attention. We were all watching that white Bronco." After receiving numerous calls from angry hoop fans, NBC settled on a surreal split-screen format for the last part of the game, broadcasting the action from Madison Square Garden on one side and the slow-motion car chase from California on the other. Memorable for reasons that had nothing to with the result, this Knicks-Rockets tilt ranks as the NBA finals game seen by the most viewers who weren't watching it.

Most TV households in one country to watch a player's NBA debut
287 million: China, Yao Ming, October 30, 2002
The NBA has millions of reasons to be excited about the Chinese TV market, a point underscored by the debut of Houston's seven-foot-six Yao Ming against the Indiana Pacers. The game, which was carried by China Central Television, reached 287 million TV households. By contrast, there are only about 105 million TV households in the United States. Although the game may have been a letdown to Yao's Chinese fans—he played just 11 minutes, had two rebounds, and didn't score in a loss—the Rockets center has since developed into a bona fide star and opened the gates to the world's largest market.

First player to have his high school games broadcast nationally

LeBron James, 2002–03

The hype machine runs amok. "King" James was on the covers of *Sports Illustrated* and *ESPN The Magazine* while still in high school, and he was already negotiating multi-million dollar shoe contracts while a senior. The attention he received was so great that his high school games were available nationally on pay-per-view and some were even televised nationally.

Most TV viewers for a regular-season game

35 million: Indiana vs. Chicago, March 19, 1995

In March 1995, Michael Jordan returned from a 17-month retirement and played in his first NBA game since Game 6 of the 1993 finals against Phoenix. In front of an excited crowd at Indiana's Market Square Arena, Air Jordan counted 19 points in 43 minutes, but the Pacers beat the Bulls in overtime 103–96. The game was televised on NBC and drew a 10.9 national rating and some 35 million viewers, making it the most-watched regular-season game in NBA history.

Most TV viewers for a playoff game

72 million: Utah vs. Chicago, June 14, 1998

Television viewers knew that Game 6 of the NBA finals might be Michael Jordan's last hurrah, and it was this curiosity as much as the drama of the finals that caused a record 72 million people to tune in. Jordan left everyone with a searing memory by hitting a game-winning jumper with 5.2 seconds left to give the Chicago Bulls their sixth championship of the 1990s.

Most consecutive NBA games called by a broadcaster

3,338: Chick Hearn, Los Angeles, 1965 to 2001

Hearn is credited with coining some of basketball's most familiar phrases, including "air ball," "It didn't draw iron," and "No harm, no foul." The popular broadcaster's longevity was even more impressive than his vocabulary. He covered the Los Angles Lakers for 42 years, including a streak of 3,338 consecutive games. The streak began in November 1965 and did not end until December 2001 when he had to undergo heart surgery.

Most famous call by an NBA broadcaster

"Havlicek stole the ball!": Johnny Most, Boston vs. Philadelphia, April 15, 1965

The Celtics were leading the 76ers 110–103 late in Game 7 of the Eastern Conference finals at Boston Garden when coach Red Auerbach lit his trademark victory cigar. But Philly rallied to make it 110–109 and was threatening to pull off a stunning upset when Hal Greer tried to inbound the ball to Chet Walker under his own basket. Celtics forward John Havlicek anticipated the move and was immortalized with Johnny Most's ear-piercing call: "Greer is putting the ball in play. He gets it out, and Havlicek steals it! Over to Sam Jones. Havlicek stole the ball! It's all over! It's allll over!" The steal kept alive the Celtics' amazing run of consecutive championships, a streak that would reach eight before the 76ers finally toppled Boston in 1967.

Shortest trademark call by an NBA broadcaster

"Yesss!": Marv Albert

Albert has several recognizable catchphrases, but the most famous is his trademark exclamation "Yesss!" when a player scores a basket. As Albert admitted in a 2003 *Sports Illustrated* interview, it wasn't an original creation. "There was an official in the NBA in the fifties named Sid Borgia. "He was a very animated official who would go through gyrations when someone scored a basket. He would say, 'Yes!,' and if a guy was fouled, 'And it counts!'" recalled Albert. "I remember early in my career during a Knicks playoff game Dick Barnett hit what was called a fallback baby jumper that banked in at the buzzer at the end of a quarter and I just happened to say, 'Yes!' People started to repeat it back to me and I started to incorporate it. It just seemed natural."

Most amusing case of mistaken broadcaster identity

Marv Albert, 1998

When Albert returned to NBA broadcasts for the first time after his 1997 conviction on a sex charge, a courtside heckler was waiting to greet him with a stream of abuse. There was only one problem: the heckler kept referring to Albert as "Brent Musburger," much to the chagrin of the real Musburger, who was broadcasting the game for ESPN radio. "I wasn't indicted," Musburger protested. "I can't relate. It's an enormous distraction."

First NBA city to acquire a nickname from an announcer's call

Portland, "Rip City," mid-1970s

Bill Schonely, the longtime voice of the Trail Blazers, coined the term "Rip City" in reference to the swish of a ball going through a basket during Portland's rise to the upper levels of the Western Conference in the mid-1970s. "He stops! He shoots! Rip City!" The phrase has since become permanently attached to Portland.

Most miles covered by a TV analyst, one playoff season
40,173: Bill Walton, 2002
On April 20, 2002, Walton embarked on a 30-day, 30-game "Love it Live!" playoff tour of America that the eccentric analyst chronicled in daily dispatches on NBA.com. Filled with rock 'n' roll references and loopy observations, the commentary was vintage Walton. In one entry he discussed Kobe Bryant's close-cropped hair. "I'm very concerned for Kobe Bryant and his new haircut. He needs to listen to some more Bob Dylan, particularly the story about growing your hair out, because if you don't, Bob warns that it stays inside and scrambles your brainwaves."

Most embarrassing prediction by an NBA analyst
Charles Barkley, November 2002
Early in the 2002–03 season TNT basketball analysts Charles Barkley and Kenny Smith made a strange bet. Ridiculing Smith for his praise of Yao Ming, Houston's seven-foot-six rookie, Barkley loudly declared that Yao would never score 19 points in a game. Barkley was so confident that he said he would kiss Smith's ass if he was proven wrong. At the time, the bet seemed a safe one; Yao had averaged just 3.3 points in his first six games. Yao must have been inspired by the put-down—three days later, he scored 20 points against the Lakers. A week later, Smith brought a donkey into the studio during their "Inside the NBA" segment to collect on the bet. With a studio panel that included Minnesota Governor Jesse

Ventura mocking him, Barkley leaned in close and gave the donkey a quick peck on the haunches.

Shortest press release to announce a comeback
2 words: Michael Jordan, Chicago, March 18, 1995

"I'm back." This was the terse press release that Jordan submitted through his agent David Falk to announce he was ending a 17-month retirement, which included a failed attempt at playing baseball. Jordan resumed his basketball career with the Chicago Bulls, whom he had earlier led to three championships. He would lead them to three more titles before retiring for a second time.

First NBA player to call a press conference to complain about being forced to practice
Allen Iverson, Philadelphia, May 7, 2002

Hey, it's hard being an NBA superstar. Just ask "The Answer." After the 76ers were beaten in the first round of the 2002 playoffs and Iverson was criticized by coach Larry Brown for repeatedly missing practices, the guard held a press conference in which he griped: "I'm supposed to be the franchise player, and we're in here talking about practice. We're not even talking about the game, the actual game, when it matters. We're talking about practice. How silly is that? I know I'm supposed to be there. I know I'm supposed to lead by example. I know it's important, but we're talking about practice. How the hell can I make my teammates better by practicing?" The diatribe gave fans a sense of the problems Brown was having instilling a team-first ethic in Philadelphia. Brown would resign a year later and take his silly practice ideas to Detroit, where he promptly led the team-concept Pistons to the NBA title.

Most obscene T-shirt slogan worn to a signing announcement

"Fuck What Ya Heard": Rasheed Wallace, Portland, 1996

Hello Portland! After obtaining Wallace in a trade with Washington, the Trail Blazers held a press conference to introduce their new power forward to local fans. The second-year pro arrived wearing a T-shirt that made him a difficult photographic subject—printed on the chest was the phrase "Fuck What Ya Heard." Presumably, this was Wallace's answer to anyone who might have had questions about his cantankerous personality.

First player to arrive for a press conference in a tractor trailer

Shaquille O'Neal, Miami, July 20, 2004

O'Neal made a striking entrance at a rally welcoming him to Miami, pulling up in a semi–tractor trailer with the words "Diesel Power" printed on the side. The seven-foot-one, 340-pound center emerged from the vehicle and began firing a plastic water cannon at the crowd of several thousand, then strode up a red carpet to the entrance of American Airlines Arena where he forecast an even larger celebration in the future. "Remember this," O'Neal told the fans. "I'm going to bring a championship to Miami. I promise."

First player to have his image airbrushed by the NBA

Allen Iverson, Philadelphia, 1999

Although Iverson is one of the NBA's most popular players, the league has always had reservations about his gangsta image. When the NBA's in-house magazine, *Hoops,* published a feature on the 76ers star in 1999, it airbrushed out Iverson's diamond earrings, neck tattoo, and necklace before putting his picture on the cover. The magazine even altered Iverson's hair, removing his cornrows and giving him a more conservative cut called a "fade." Iverson was unhappy with the makeover. "The photo was an insult, terrible. I wish they wouldn't use me at all if they can't accept all of me. I have things on my body that are just tattoos to others but mean a lot to me, about my mother, my grandmother, my kids, my fiancée. These aren't just tattoos to me."

First NBA owner to host a TV reality show

Mark Cuban, The Benefactor, 2004

In a bid to copy the success of Donald Trump's *The Apprentice,* the Dallas Mavericks owner starred in an ABC reality show called *The Benefactor.* Sixteen contestants competed against one another in a series of goofy challenges with the ultimate winner receiving a million dollars. The reviewers were not kind. Glenn Garvin of the *Miami Herald* wrote: "It rewards the willingness of people to submit to the totalitarian whims of an all-powerful control freak. It's like a game-show version of a Nazi concentration camp." *The Benefactor* attracted few viewers and was quickly canceled.

First former NBA player to win a TV reality show

Dennis Rodman, Celebrity Mole Yucatan, 2004

Considering that Rodman was in the cast, it probably should have been called *Celebrity Worm Yucatan.* Rodman and some B-actors competed against one another for $222,000. The former rebounding specialist won by correctly identifying Angie Everhart as the mole. Despite taking no notes throughout the series, Rodman somehow answered 17 of 20 questions correctly on the final quiz.

[14]

THE
WINNER'S
CIRCLE

Bill Russell is the only NBA player with more championship rings than he has fingers. Unlike other superstars, who tend to be remembered for their individual skills, Russell became synonymous with winning. The Celtics great captured 11 titles in his 13-year career.

Most Game 7 wins in playoffs, career
10: Bill Russell, 1956–57 to 1968–69
Statistically speaking, Russell usually came out second-best to his great rival Wilt Chamberlain, but not in the stat that mattered most. Russell won 11 NBA titles to Chamberlain's two, and was an incredible 10–0 in Game 7 during his storied career. Of the 10, eight were won in Boston and two on the road, and five came in the NBA finals.

Most playoff games without winning a championship, career
193: Karl Malone, 1984–85 to 2004–05
Malone's career was studded with personal accomplishments, including 11 first-team All-Star selections, three All-Defensive first team selections, and two MVP awards, but the man that many consider the game's greatest power forward never won the big award—an NBA title. Malone retired in 2005 with 36,928 career points, second only to Kareem Abdul-Jabbar.

Most finals played in without winning a championship, career
7: Elgin Baylor, 1958–59 to 1971–72
So close, yet so far. Baylor reached the NBA finals seven times with the Lakers during his 14-year career, only to come out on the losing end each time. It's hard to argue that his play had much to do with the futility streak: he averaged 27.0 points and 12.9 rebounds per game in 134 playoff matches. Two games into the 1970–71 season, the sweet-shooting forward went down with a knee injury that all but ended his career. He missed the rest of the campaign and returned for only nine games in 1971–72 before retiring at age 37. Ironically, the day after Baylor retired, with Jim McMillian

replacing him in the lineup, the Lakers began a 33-game winning streak that is the longest in pro sports history. Later that season, Los Angeles won the championship.

Most brazen playoff prediction

Four consecutive sweeps: Moses Malone, Philadelphia, April 1983
After going 65–17 in 1982–83, the Philadelphia 76ers were favored to win the crown, but even so, Malone pushed the envelope. When asked before the start of the playoffs how his team would do, the MVP center replied in his Virginia vernacular, "Fo', Fo', Fo'," meaning three straight sweeps. The 76ers almost fulfilled the prediction. They went 12–1 in the postseason, beating the Knicks in four, the Bucks in five, and then crushing the defending champion Lakers in four straight games in the finals. An amended version of Malone's boast was engraved on the 76ers' championship rings. It read: "Fo', Fi', Fo'."

Most points scored while wearing a mask, one postseason

494: Richard Hamilton, Detroit, 2004
Hamilton fractured his nose early in the 2003–04 season, and then had it broken again in February, which led to nasal reconstructive surgery. If he had any hope of remaining on the active roster for the NBA playoffs he had to wear a protective mask. Hamilton, who was initially reluctant to don the clear Hannibal Lecter–like face-gear, later claimed that wearing it improved his shooting focus. He led Detroit with a 21.5 points per game average in the 2004 playoffs and continued to wear it in 2004–05.

Most points scored, one playoff series

284: Elgin Baylor, Los Angeles, 1962

The Lakers forward was simply unstoppable in the 1962 finals, scoring 284 points against the Boston Celtics in the seven-game series. Baylor's lowest point total of the seven contests came in the sixth game, when he scored *only* 34 points in a 119–105 loss. Even though he poured in 41 points in the seventh game at Boston, his team lost a heart-breaker in overtime, 110–107.

Most consecutive 40-point games, one series

6: Jerry West, Los Angeles, 1965

During the 1960s, the Lakers boasted the league's deadliest scoring duo in Elgin Baylor and Jerry West. The pair, known as Mr. Inside and Mr. Outside because of their preferred shooting styles, averaged a combined 58 points per game in 1964–65. But when Baylor blew out his knee in Game 1 of the Western Division finals against the Baltimore Bullets, the burden fell on Mr. Outside. West responded by scoring 49, 52, 44, 48, 43, and 42 points in the six games of the series to propel the Lakers to the NBA finals. His 46.3 points-per-game average for the series has never been surpassed.

Highest percentage of a team's points,
one playoff game (minimum 40 points)

55.7: Allen Iverson, Philadelphia, May 9, 2001

The Answer showed why he was voted league MVP in a 97–92 win over Toronto in Game 2 of the 2001 Eastern Conference semifinals. After Philadelphia lost the opening game of the series at home to the Raptors, it faced a must-win situation in Game 2. Iverson carried his team to victory,

tallying 19 straight points in the fourth quarter to finish
with 54 for the game. That was 55.7 percent of the 76ers'
offense, an NBA playoff record.

Highest percentage of a team's
points, one finals game (minimum 40 points)
51.7: Michael Jordan, Chicago, June 14, 1998
Jordan was the ultimate closer. With Chicago trailing Utah
by three points in the final minute, Jordan scored on a drive.
Then he stripped the ball from Karl Malone at the defensive
end, came down the floor and buried a 20-foot jumper with
5.2 seconds left, to give the Bulls an 87–86 victory and their
sixth NBA title in eight years. Jordan shot 15-of-35 from the
field and 12-of-15 from the line and scored 16 points in the
fourth quarter, including Chicago's final eight over the last
2:06. He finished with 45 points, over half of the Bulls' total
offense. The last bucket gave him this record. "Let's face it,"
said Bulls guard Steve Kerr, "we all hopped on Michael's
back. He just carried us. It was his game tonight. He is so
good it's scary."

Most points scored with a sprained ankle, one quarter
25: Isiah Thomas, Detroit, June 19, 1988
The Pistons trailed 56–48 early in the third quarter of Game
6 of the 1988 finals when Thomas scored 14 consecutive
points in rapid succession: two free throws, a five-footer off
an offensive rebound, followed by four jumpers, a bank shot,
and a layup. Then, with about four minutes to go in the period, Thomas landed awkwardly on Michael Cooper's foot
and had to be helped from the floor. Despite a severely
sprained ankle, he returned 35 seconds later and continued

his assault. By the end of the quarter, the Pistons guard had hit 11-of-13 shots from the floor for 25 points, setting a finals record for a quarter. Thomas finished with 43 points, eight assists, and six steals, but not a victory. The Lakers won 103–102.

Most points scored with two dislocated fingers, one game
44: Bernard King, New York, April 27, 1984
King was a fireball in the Knicks' 1984 first-round clash with Detroit, averaging 42.6 points per game in the best-of-five series on 60 percent shooting. In the fifth game he knocked down 44 points despite wearing splints on the middle fingers of each hand, both of which had been dislocated. Yet Detroit's Isiah Thomas nearly upstaged him. New York led by eight with 1:57 remaining when Thomas reeled off 16 points in 94 seconds to send the game to overtime. New York finally won 127–123.

Most points scored in a playoff loss
63: Michael Jordan, Chicago, April 20, 1986
Jordan played just 18 regular-season games in his second year in the NBA, after breaking a small bone in his foot in Chicago's third game. Although he was encouraged to sit out the entire season to make sure he was fully healed, Jordan insisted on coming back late in the schedule, and he led the Bulls to the 1986 playoffs. It was in Game 2 of Chicago's first-round match against the eventual NBA champion Boston Celtics that Jordan showed just how thoroughly he had recovered. In the hallowed halls of the Boston Garden, he set a playoff record by scoring an amazing 63 points against what many consider to be one of the greatest NBA

teams ever. The Celtics won the game 135–131 in double overtime and went on to sweep the Bulls, but Jordan's record still stands. After the game, Boston's Larry Bird marveled at the youngster's awesome performance, stating, "I think that was just God disguised as Michael Jordan."

Best performance in a finals game by a player suffering from stomach flu

Michael Jordan, Chicago, June 11, 1997

Jordan was stricken with a virus the night before Game 5 of the 1997 finals in Salt Lake City. With MJ lying in the darkened trainer's room before the game, the Bulls locker room was deathly silent. "I've played a lot of seasons with Michael and I've never seen him so sick," said Scottie Pippen. Despite being badly dehydrated, Jordan played 44 minutes and scored 38 points, including a pivotal three-pointer with 25 seconds left. He added seven rebounds, five assists, three steals, and one blocked shot as the Bulls defeated Utah 90–88 to take a 3–2 series lead. They wrapped up the title in Chicago two nights later.

Most points scored, one finals game

61: Elgin Baylor, Los Angeles, April 14, 1962

More than 40 years have passed and no one has surpassed Baylor's offensive explosion in Game 5 of the 1962 finals against the Celtics. Making the feat even more impressive, he did it on the road in the hostile din of Boston Garden. Baylor was guarded in the game by Tom "Satch" Sanders, a defensive specialist. If Baylor got past Sanders he then had to contend with Bill Russell, merely the best defensive player of all time. The Lakers gunner hit 24-of-46 shots from the floor and scored 61 points to key a 126–121 victory.

Most points scored in a finals game by a player with a broken wrist
22: George Mikan, Minneapolis, April 11, 1949
The Washington Capitols thought they caught a break when Mikan fractured his hand in Game 4 of the 1949 NBA finals. But the Lakers star refused to let the injury sideline him. Mikan played Game 5 with a cast on his hand and still pumped in 22 points, even though Washington prevailed 74–65. Game 6 was played on the Lakers' home court and Mikan's team came away with a 77–56 win and the championship. Washington's Horace "Bones" McKinney, who had the task of guarding Mikan in the finals recalled, "He wore a cast that was hard as a brick. It fit right in with his elbows. It would kill you. And it didn't bother his shooting a bit."

Most poorly timed display of dribbling in a playoff game
Derek Harper, Dallas, May 6, 1984
A glance at the scoreboard would have helped. There were six seconds left in Game 4 of the Western Conference semifinals between the Lakers and the Mavericks and the score was tied when Harper rebounded the ball. Unfortunately, the Dallas rookie thought his team had a one-point lead and, despite the desperate cries of his teammates (and 20,000 Mavericks fans), he triumphantly dribbled out the clock without taking a shot. Given a second chance, the Lakers won the contest in overtime, 122–115, then captured the series in the next game.

Most petulant act in the last seconds of a playoff game
A sit-down strike: Scottie Pippen, Chicago, May 13, 1994
Michael Jordan's retirement in 1994 put the spotlight on the
Bulls' second banana, Scottie Pippen, and he did not handle
it well. With 1.8 seconds left in a tie game during the Eastern Conference semifinals against the Knicks, Chicago called
time. Coach Phil Jackson devised a play on the sidelines that
would set up Toni Kukoc for a potential game-winning shot.
But when Pippen heard that he would not be taking the shot,
he sat down and refused to go back on the court. Chicago ran
Jackson's play and Kukoc sank the buzzer beater.

Most ingenious last-second strategy in a playoff game
Calling an illegal time-out: Paul Westphal,
Phoenix, June 4, 1976
Some call it the most exciting game ever played. Game 5 of
the 1976 NBA finals between the tradition-steeped Boston
Celtics and the upstart Phoenix Suns lasted three overtimes
and had enough thrills and twists for an entire series. In the
second overtime, Phoenix led by one point with four seconds
left, but Boston's John Havlicek raced the length of the floor
and scored on a 15-foot bank shot that brought hundreds of
hysterical Celtics fans pouring onto the fabled parquet. Only
one problem—there was still one second left to play. As the
floor was being cleared, Paul Westphal came up with an
ingenious idea. Because the Suns were to get the ball at the
endline with one second and no chance to move the ball in
range for a shot, he called a time-out, which was illegal since
Phoenix had no time-outs left. The Celtics were awarded
a foul shot, which Jo Jo White sank, putting them up
112–110. But now the Suns got the ball at midcourt. They

inbounded to forward Gar Heard, who caught the pass, turned and swished through a 20-foot jumper at the buzzer to stun the crowd and send the game into a third overtime. But Westphal's skulduggery ultimately proved futile, as Boston prevailed in triple overtime 128–126. Two days later, Boston beat the Suns 87–80 in Phoenix to claim the crown.

Most positions played, one finals game

5: Magic Johnson, Los Angeles, May 16, 1980

When the Lakers flew to Philadelphia for Game 6 of the 1980 finals most people expected they would be returning to California for Game 7. Kareem Abdul-Jabbar, the league's most dominant player, had injured his ankle in Game 5 and did not make the trip. But the Lakers had a magic trick up their sleeves—Magic Johnson, that is. Starting the game at Jabbar's center spot, the 20-year-old rookie turned in a stunning show, scoring 42 points, collecting 15 boards, seven assists, and three steals. At times, he seemed to be everywhere. In fact, Johnson played all five positions—center, point guard, shooting guard, small forward, and power forward—in the game, as he led the Lakers to a 123–107 championship-clinching win. Afterward coach Paul Westhead said of his amazing rookie: "We all thought he was a movie-star player, but we found out he wears a hard hat. It's like finding a great orthopedic surgeon who can also operate a bulldozer."

Only player from a losing team to win a finals MVP

Jerry West, Los Angeles, 1969

West enjoyed great individual success, but his playoff record with Los Angeles was a study in disappointment. In nine seasons from 1962 to 1970 the Lakers made the finals six times, losing to Boston five times and to New York once. Three of the series went seven games, with the Lakers losing two of them to the Celtics by a single basket. In Game 7 of the 1969 finals, West played with a leg injury and collected 42 points, 13 rebounds, and 12 assists—yet still came out a loser. The performance moved Celtics center Bill Russell to say, "Los Angeles has not won the championship, but Jerry West is a champion." West was voted MVP of the finals, the only player from a losing team to cop the honor.

Best verbal barb in a finals game

"The Mailman doesn't deliver on Sunday":
Scottie Pippen, Chicago, June 1, 1997

The game was on a Sunday and it ended when Michael Jordan scored at the buzzer to give the Chicago Bulls an 84–82 victory over the Utah Jazz in the first game of the 1997 finals. The ending neatly wrapped up all the pre-series hype over who was more deserving of the 1997 MVP award—Karl Malone, who won it, or Jordan, who finished second. Jordan finished the game with 31 points on 13-of-27 shooting with eight assists and four rebounds. Malone, who missed seven of his first eight shots from the field, had 23 points and 15 rebounds. However, his inability to make two free throws with nine seconds left was a crippler for Utah. Just before Malone stepped to the line to take his free shots, Scottie Pippen leaned over and said something. With a sellout United Center crowd screaming its lungs out, Malone rolled the first one off the rim and then did the same with the second. After the game, Pippen was asked what he said to Malone. "I told him, 'The Mailman doesn't deliver on Sunday.'"

Most spectacular layup in a finals game

Julius Erving, Philadelphia, May 10, 1980

The final score is long forgotten. The only thing that
is clearly remembered about Game 1 of the 1980 finals is
Dr. J's impossible, gravity-defying layup. Early in the fourth
quarter Erving drove past Laker defender Mark Landsberger
and toward the basket along the right baseline. When
towering seven-foot-two Kareeem Abdul-Jabbar stepped
into his path, Dr. J swung his right arm—and the basketball—behind the backboard, and floated past Abdul-Jabbar.
Suspended in the air, Erving somehow slid his body just
enough to the left so that he could reach his right arm back
toward the basket and then, using backspin, flip in a layup.
The Philadelphia crowd was momentarily stunned into
silence before erupting into cheers. "I could not believe my
eyes," said Magic Johnson. "It's still the greatest move I've
ever seen in basketball. The all-time greatest."

Most inspiring pair of baskets scored in a finals game

Willis Reed, New York, May 8, 1970

When Reed tore a thigh muscle in Game 5 of the 1970
finals, the Knicks championship hopes looked grim. The six-
foot-nine center had carried the team in the first four games
of the series, scoring 37, 29, 38, and 23 points respectively,
while averaging 15 rebounds. Although the Knicks gutted
out a win in Game 5 without Reed, they were demolished
by the Lakers in Game 6, and Knicks fans feared a repeat in
Game 7 if Reed couldn't play. After receiving several
pain-killing injections in his thigh, Reed limped onto the
court just before game time. The crowd at Madison Square
Garden went wild and his teammates' confidence surged.

Reed somehow managed to outjump Wilt Chamberlain on the opening tip, then scored the game's first basket on a shot from the top of the key. He then scored the second New York basket from 20 feet out. Although he didn't score again, Reed defused Chamberlain's shooting and New York took control of the game. The Knicks went on to win 113–99 to capture their first NBA title.

Longest buzzer-beater in a finals game
60 feet: Jerry West, Los Angeles, April 29, 1970
They didn't call West "Mr. Clutch" for nothing. He lived to take the big shot. Look no further than Game 3 of the 1970 finals. The Knicks looked to have it won when Dave DeBusschere made a bucket with three seconds left to give New York a 102–100 edge. Out of time-outs, Los Angeles inbounded to West, who launched a miracle shot from beyond midcourt. It found net. Unfortunately for the Lakers, the NBA didn't have a three-point shot at that time, so the game went to overtime where the Knicks regrouped to win 111–108. "It was a beautiful thing wasted," said West.

First team to blame a finals loss on a Gatorade mixup
Chicago Bulls, June 8, 1997
After Utah downed Chicago 78–73 in Game 4 of the 1997 finals, the Bulls blamed the loss on a team assistant, who became confused and mistakenly served Gatorlode to the players instead of Gatorade. Gatorlode, a drink rich in carbohydrates, is supposed to be consumed after a game. As a result, it was as if the Chicago players had eaten 20 baked potatoes a piece. Michael Jordan and Scottie Pippen suffered stomach cramps and Dennis Rodman had to run off the floor

to use the bathroom. Chicago's head trainer, Chip Schaefer, didn't discover the error until late in the game and by then it was too late.

Most home games in the finals
moved because of a bowling tournament
3: Fort Wayne Pistons, 1955

The NBA didn't have the same clout in the 1950s as it does today. Case in point: the 1955 finals between the Fort Wayne Pistons and the Syracuse Nationals. For years the Pistons had played their games at Fort Wayne's North Side High School, until owner Fred Zollner finally convinced the city to build a new arena in 1952. But few people figured that the Pistons would ever be good enough to make it to the finals, and so Memorial Coliseum scheduled another event, the American Bowling Congress Tournament, for the first week of April 1955. That created a conflict with the Pistons' home dates in the finals and the club was forced to shift its three home games to Indianapolis, where the team had only a marginal following. Although Fort Wayne won all three, it lost the series in seven games. The experience so frustrated Zollner that he vowed to shift the franchise to Detroit, eventually making the move in 1957.

Most unsportsmanlike gesture by a team in a Conference final
Detroit Pistons, May 27, 1991

Entering the 1991 playoffs, the swaggering Pistons had won back-to-back NBA titles and had beaten Chicago three straight years in the Eastern Conference playoffs. But the "Bad Boys" reign came to a humiliating end as the Bulls trampled the Pistons in four games, completing the sweep with a 115–94 rout in Motown. With eight seconds left in Game 4, Isiah Thomas and the other Detroit starters left their seats on the bench and walked off the court, and with the exception of John Salley, refused to congratulate the Bulls afterward.

Most premature postgame celebration in a finals
Los Angeles Lakers, May 5, 1969
Before Game 7 of the 1969 NBA finals, Boston's Bill Russell got his hands on a script that described plans for a postgame Lakers celebration that included a rendition of "Happy Days Are Here Again" to be played by the University of Southern Caifornia band. When the Celtics walked out on the court to begin the game against the heavily favored Lakers, they saw 5,000 balloons suspended in nets from the ceiling. But as was often the case during that era, the Celtics found a way to win. Don Nelson's late jumper, which bounded off the back rim straight up into the air and down into the basket, was the key to a 108–106 victory. The triumph gave the Celtics their 11th title in 13 years.

Most combined regular-season wins of
teams defeated in the playoffs by a champion
238: Houston Rockets, 1994–95
Hakeem Olajuwon and the Rockets were defending champs, so it seems a misnomer to call them underdogs, but based on the regular season that's exactly what they were. The Rockets finished sixth in the West with a 47–35 mark. But the club improved itself with a mid-season trade for Olajuwon's college teammate, Clyde "the Glide" Drexler. With the dangerous duo riding shotgun, the Rockets did something no other

team has ever done: knock off four 55-plus win opponents. Houston beat Utah (60–22), Phoenix (59–23), San Antonio (62–20), and Orlando (57–25) to take the crown.

Most consecutive series losses in the finals
8: Minneapolis/Los Angeles Lakers, 1959 to 1970
The Lakers copped five rings in six trips to the finals in Minneapolis, but after the club moved to California in 1960, winning it all suddenly became an impossible chore. Despite being the class of the West, the Lakers consistently came up short against their Eastern nemesis, the Boston Celtics, who beat the Lakers in seven straight finals between 1959 and 1969. When Los Angeles finally met a different foe in the 1970 finals—the New York Knicks—the result was the same. Finally, in 1972, the Lakers ended the Eastern jinx, beating the Knicks in the finals.

Largest fourth-quarter comeback in a playoff game
21 points: Boston vs. New Jersey, May 25, 2002
Leading 74 to 53 after three quarters, the Nets appeared to have Game 3 of the Eastern Conference finals sewn up. In NBA playoff history, 171 teams had taken leads of more than 18 points into the last quarter and none had lost. New Jersey's reserves were so confident they were laughing at the Celtics. But the grins vanished when Boston staged a frantic rally. Leading the charge was Paul Pierce, who scored 19 of his team-high 28 points in the quarter as the Celtics outscored the Nets 41 to 16 in the final 12 minutes to post a 94–90 victory. Although the miracle comeback gave the Celtics a 2–1 lead in the series, they had shot their bolt. They dropped the next three games and were eliminated.

Fewest total points scored in a playoff game (since the advent of the shot clock)

130: Boston vs. Detroit, May 10, 2002

There was a whole lot of clanging going on. Neither the Celtics nor the Pistons could find the basket, each hitting just 35 percent of their shots in a Celtics 66–64 victory in Game 3 of the 2002 Eastern Conference semifinals. The teams were even worse from the three-point range, shooting a combined 4-for-39. Boston was 2-for-19; Detroit was 2-for-20. But Boston's coach Jim O'Brien didn't care what the game looked like. "It's not a dance theater," he said. "If you get a W, you go home with a big grin on your face."

Largest total margin of victory, one playoff series

95 points: Los Angeles vs. San Antonio, 1986

Believe it or not, this slaughter occurred in a three-game series. Showing no mercy, Pat Riley's glitter brigade destroyed Cotton Fitzsimmons's Spurs by scores of 135–88, 122–94, and 114–94.

Largest margin of victory in a playoff game

58 points: Minneapolis vs. St. Louis, March 19, 1956

The Lakers outscored St. Louis 363 to 307 in the three-game Western Division semifinals in 1956, yet still lost the series. The Hawks won Game 1 116–115 at home, then traveled to Minneapolis where they were pummeled 133–75 by the Lakers, setting a record for the most lopsided loss in a playoff game. Hawks coach Red Holzman must have made some key adjustments after Game 2, because two nights later in Minneapolis, the Hawks took the series with another 116–115 win.

Largest margin of victory in a playoff road win

56 points: Los Angeles at Golden State, April 21, 1973

Golden State had upset the top-seeded Milwaukee Bucks in the first round of the 1973 playoffs, but the Warriors could not contain Wilt Chamberlain, Jerry West, Gail Goodrich, and the rest of the Lakers in the Western Conference finals. In Game 3, at the Oakland Coliseum, the Lakers crushed Golden State 126–70. The Warriors set an NBA record for shooting futility in the game, sinking just 27 of 116 shots, a pathetic .233 percentage.

Largest margin of victory, one finals game

42 points: Chicago vs. Utah, June 7, 1998

Imagine shelling out a couple of hundred smackers to see this travesty. Every Bull scored in the 96–54 pounding as Michael Jordan sat out the entire fourth quarter. Karl Malone was 8-for-11 from the field, but the rest of the Jazz shot 13-for-59. Utah committed a ghastly 26 turnovers and scored the fewest points by a team in a playoff game since 1950. "This will go down in Chicago history with the other big massacres, like the Valentine's Day Massacre and all the rest of them," exclaimed Utah forward Adam Keefe.

ACKNOWLEDGMENTS

Thanks to the following publications for their statistical and biographical information: *Total Basketball: The Ultimate Basketball Encyclopedia; The 2004–05 Official NBA Guide; The Official NBA Encyclopedia; The Best Book of Basketball Facts and Stats; The Encyclopedia of Pro Basketball Team Histories* by Peter C. Bjarkman; *Tall Tales: The Glory Years of the NBA* by Terry Pluto; *Out of Bounds: Inside the NBA's Culture of Rape, Violence, and Crime* by Jeff Benedict; *Who's Better, Who's Best in Basketball?* by Elliott Kalb; *The Night Wilt Scored 100: Tales from Basketball's Past* by Eric Nagel; *Playing for Keeps: Michael Jordan and the World He Made* by David Halberstam.

The author is also indebted to numerous Web sites, including NBAcom; ESPN.com; CNNSI.com; basketball reference.com; centurysports.net/basketball; hoopshype.com; hoopsvibe.com; sportsencylopedia.com; shrpsports.com; thesmokingun.com; cracksmoker.com; badjocks.com; and anecdotage.com

The author gratefully acknowledges the help of Rob Sanders, Susan Rana, Ruth Wilson, Peter Cocking, Jessica Sullivan, and Chris Labonte at Greystone Books and also Judith Anderson and David Peterman.

INDEX